S0-AEH-388

# Slavery in Colonial America, 1619–1776

USED BOOK
College Store
Sacramento City College
Sell your books on campus
during finals

USED BOOK
College Store
Sacramento City College
Sell your books on campus
during finals

# The African American History Series

Series Editors:
Jacqueline M. Moore, Austin College
Nina Mjagkij, Ball State University

This series, which takes both chronological and thematic approaches to topics and individuals crucial to an understanding of the African American experience, is an attempt to address that problem. The books in this series, in lively prose by established scholars, are aimed primarily at nonspecialists. They focus on topics in African American history that have broad significance and place them in their historical context. While presenting sophisticated interpretations based on primary sources and the latest scholarship, the authors tell their stories in a succinct manner, avoiding jargon and obscure language. They include selected documents that allow readers to judge the evidence for themselves and to evaluate the authors' conclusions. Bridging the gap between popular and academic history, these books bring the African American story to life.

**Volumes Published**

*Booker T. Washington, W.E.B. Du Bois, and the Struggle for Racial Uplift*
    Jacqueline M. Moore
*Slavery in Colonial America, 1619(1776*
    Betty Wood

**Forthcoming**

*African Americans and the Labor Movement*
    Brian Kelly
*African Americans in the Jazz Age*
*A Decade of Struggle and Promise*
    Marc Schneider
*The African American Experience in Vietnam*
    James Westheider
*Bayard Rustin*
*American Dreamer*
    Jerald Podair
*The Montgomery Bus Boycott*
    John White
*Plantation Slave Life*
    Larry Hudson

# Slavery in Colonial America, 1619–1776

Betty Wood

ROWMAN & LITTLEFIELD PUBLISHERS, INC.
Lanham • Boulder • New York • Toronto • Oxford

ROWMAN & LITTLEFIELD PUBLISHERS, INC.

Published in the United States of America
by Rowman & Littlefield Publishers, Inc.
A wholly owned subsidary of The Rowman & Littlefield Publishing Group, Inc.
4501 Forbes Boulevard, Suite 200, Lanham, Maryland 20706
www.rowmanlittlefield.com

PO Box 317
Oxford
OX2 9RU, UK

Copyright © 2005 by Rowman & Littlefield Publishers, Inc.

*All rights reserved.* No part of this publication may be reproduced,
stored in a retrieval system, or transmitted in any form or by any
means, electronic, mechanical, photocopying, recording, or otherwise,
without the prior permission of the publisher.

British Library Cataloguing in Publication Information Available

**Library of Congress Cataloging-in-Publication Data**

Wood, Betty.
    Slavery in colonial America, 1619–1776 / Betty Wood.
        p.   cm.— (The African American history series)
    Includes bibliographical references and index.
    ISBN 0-7425-4418-4 (cloth : alk. paper)—ISBN 0-7425-4419-2 (pbk. : alk. paper)
        1. Slavery—United States—History—17th century.   2. Slavery—United
    States—History—18th century.   3. United States—History—Colonial period, ca.
    1600–1775.   4. African Americans—History—To 1863.   5. Plantation life—United
    States—History—17th century.   6. Plantation life—United States—History—18th
    century.   I. Title.   II. Series: African American history series (Wilmington, Del.)
    E446.W88 2005
    306.3'62'097309032—dc22                                        2004024938

Printed in the United States of America

∞ ™ The paper used in this publication meets the minimum requirements of American
National Standard for Information Sciences—Permanence of Paper for Printed Library
Materials, ANSI/NISO Z39.48-1992.

# Contents

~

# Introduction

Until quite recently, and especially when compared with the amount written about slavery and race relations during the thirty or so years before the Civil War, the emergence and development of slavery in early British America was much neglected. For a long time those scholars who did specialize in this area were interested mainly in why it was that, at different times in different places, the colonists decided that people of African ancestry were suitable candidates for enslavement. Some historians believed that the answer lay in a deep-seated racism that the early British colonists took with them to North America. Others took a different view, and argued that the introduction of slavery had more to do with economics—with trying to secure the cheapest and most productive workers—than it did with a racial ideology that, at worst, doubted the very humanity of west and west central African peoples.

Much of this older research focused on the beginnings of slavery in Virginia, England's first American colony, and was more interested in those doing the enslaving than in those being enslaved. More recent studies have looked in closer detail at the other mainland colonies and have brought enslaved people to center stage by examining the different experiences of slavery from their perspectives. This book, which is intended for those coming to the subject for the first time, will examine the main themes that have emerged from this new research.

We begin by examining the ways in which racial ideologies, religious beliefs, and economic self-interest interacted in the different physical environments of the North American mainland to produce systems of slavery that were both similar and dissimilar. During the seventeenth century, everywhere in British America, African people came to be legally defined as chattels, as pieces of property, but in Puritan New England they were also recognized as persons who were entitled to certain legal rights. As we shall also see, geography also played a key role in determining the different systems of slavery that emerged in the North American mainland. In New England, for example, relatively few people were needed to work that region's family farms, and it was mainly for that reason that black slavery never took a firm hold there. Further south, in places such as Virginia and South Carolina, the commercial production of crops such as tobacco and rice came to be seen as depending upon the use of large groups of enslaved workers. Planters came to be convinced that Africans were cheaper to keep and could be made to work much harder than Europeans.

New England and the Middle Atlantic colonies of New York, Pennsylvania, and New Jersey were never as dependent upon slave labor as were the southern colonies. However, merchants in northern towns such as New York, Philadelphia, and Newport, Rhode Island, as well as British traders, made a great deal of money by supplying African workers to southern planters via the transatlantic slave trade. In chapter 2 we examine the horrendous conditions under which thousands of west and west central African peoples were transported across the Atlantic Ocean to the North American mainland during the colonial period. A great many men, women, and children died on board the slave ships—we will never know the exact number—and those who survived found themselves being sold like cattle once they reached the port towns of British America.

More often than not brutally separated from their families and friends, these newly enslaved people found themselves being put to various kinds of work by their colonial owners. In our third chapter, we look at the working lives of slaves. Most enslaved people, women as well as men, young and old alike, became agricultural workers. But in every colony some were employed as domestic servants and others worked at different jobs in the colonial towns. Some occupations were determined by the slave's sex. For example, whether in town or countryside, most skilled trades, such as blacksmithing and carpentry, were limited to men.

Recent research has shown that enslaved people did not submit unconditionally to the demands being made of them by their owners, and in our next three chapters we investigate the different ways in which they asserted themselves. Often looking back to Africa for guidance, they tried to re-create familiar, and comforting, patterns of family and religious life in what for most were their strange new American surroundings. Given that enslaved people were brought to America from different parts of west and west central Africa, this often meant a mixing of social and religious traditions.

Battling against the most daunting odds, for example, the constant risk of being forcibly and permanently separated from their loved ones, enslaved women and men married, they had children, and they developed their own semiprivate household economies. As owners were forced to acknowledge, it was the slave family, and the supportive kinship networks that developed over time, that mattered more than anything else to enslaved people.

For much of the colonial period, slave owners paid little attention to either the family lives or the religious beliefs and practices of enslaved people unless they thought their own interests were being threatened. For their part, enslaved people were largely indifferent, or positively hostile, to the Christian beliefs of their owners. True, some slaves were converted to Christianity, but through the first half of the eighteenth century most resisted attempts to persuade them to abandon their traditional African religions. Everywhere in the mainland, this began to change during the 1740s and 1750s with the preaching of a more evangelical form of Protestantism. With its emphasis on self-worth, personal agency, and spiritual equality evangelical Protestantism appealed to slaves in a way that the more traditional forms of the Anglican, Congregationalist, and Presbyterian churches did not. As the American Revolution approached, a growing number of enslaved people, throughout the mainland colonies, were beginning to embrace the Methodist and Baptist faiths. These years witnessed the birth of African American Christianity.

Enslaved people asserted themselves not only by claiming the right to enjoy family and religious lives, but also by expressing themselves in different ways. For example, they expressed themselves and their individuality in the way they did their hair and in the clothing they wore. They verbally insulted their owners and other whites, if not always to their faces then in the semi-privacy of the slave quarters. Some expressed their defiance, and their rage, in what to their owners and white society generally was far more threatening behavior. Many ran away—sometimes to be reunited with loved ones from whom they had been forcibly separated and sometimes for other reasons. Others, knowing full well that it was almost certain to result in their own death if they were caught, physically attacked their owners and other whites with whatever weapon they had at hand. This might be an axe, a hoe or, what southern planters came to fear most of all, poison.

The one thing that it was virtually impossible for enslaved people to do on their own was to organize a rebellion on a scale that would topple white society and thereby bring about an end to their bondage. But this did now stop some from trying, even though they knew full well that the odds were so heavily stacked against them. There were two serious black uprisings in

New York, in 1712 and 1741, and in 1739 South Carolina was rocked by the Stono Rebellion. These three revolts, the most serious of the entire colonial period, were put down with comparative ease by the white authorities and those black people known, or simply thought, to have been involved in them were executed.

As we see in our final chapter, it would have taken a political sea-change on a scale unimaginable for much of the colonial period to have brought about an ending to slavery and the transatlantic slave trade. Before the 1750s and 1760s few white people, either in Britain or in the mainland American colonies, questioned the continuance of either slavery or the slave trade; by the early 1770s the abolition of both these things no longer seemed beyond the realms of possibility. The first important challenges to slavery and the slave trade came from within the Quaker communities of Pennsylvania and New Jersey. But it would take something else—the serious political crisis that developed between Britain and the American colonies during the 1760s and early 1770s—to force these issues into the forefront of the colonial American consciousness.

By the late 1760s the question was clear enough: Could the American Patriots who were demanding their own freedom, and resting their case for that freedom on the natural rights and equality of all mankind, legitimately continue to hold around 20 percent of the colonial population in perpetual, heritable slavery? In some ways, the answers to that question, and the sectional differences that would continue to plague America for decades to come, were already evident by the early 1770s.

To the wealthy rice planters of South Carolina and Georgia, it was simply unthinkable that slavery should ever be brought to an end. They, and their spokesmen, sprang to its defense. To them, slavery was not a religious, moral, or social evil but a positive, and necessary, good. Virginia planters, on the other hand, acknowledged some of the criticisms of slavery and the slave trade, but could not bring themselves to abolish slavery. As the Imperial crisis deepened during the mid-1770s, these attitudes could not be easily ignored by colonial politicians as they tried to present a united front to the British government. It was clear that compromise would have to be the order of the day, and this was the path chosen by the Patriot leaders. As the political crisis escalated into all-out war, it was now even more essential that South Carolina and Georgia be kept on board, and this meant acknowledging their strongly held views on slavery.

With their smaller numbers of enslaved people, and fewer and less politically influential slave owners, the New England and Middle Atlantic colonies appeared to be the most fertile ground for the opponents of slavery and, over the next few years, this proved to be the case. Slavery would be brought to an end in the North—in some states as soon as they declared their independence from Britain, but in others, such as Pennsylvania and New Jersey, the process would be far more gradual and far more grudging.

Initially, enslaved people in the southern colonies might well have taken heart from the political language of their Patriot owners, their talk of liberty and equality, but it could not have been long before they realized that this language did not, and in all likelihood never would, apply to them. But by the end of 1775, they were given some glimmer of hope that their freedom might come from another quarter: from the British.

Few in Britain were opposed to slavery or the transatlantic slave trade—far from it—but the British were determined to do everything in their power to quell the American Revolution. If this meant finding an active role for blacks, and even arming some of them, and giving them their freedom if they survived their tour of duty, then so be it.

The War for American Independence, then, would be not only a war that was about slavery but also a war in which large numbers of enslaved people participated in an attempt to determine their own future. The outcome of that war, and the political settlements of the 1780s, would help to seal the fate of African Americans for decades to come.

# Chronology

1750:        Black slavery permitted in Georgia

1765–1766: The Stamp Act Crisis

1770:        Crispus Attucks dies as a result of the "Boston Massacre"

1773:        Benjamin Rush publishes a pamphlet opposing slavery

1773:        The publication of a volume of Phillis Wheatley's poetry

1774:        The publication of John Woolman's *Journal*

1775:        Bernard Romans publishes a reply to Benjamin Rush in which he strongly defends black slavery

1775:        Thomas Paine attacks black slavery

1775:        Lord Dunmore offers freedom to male slaves willing to fight on the British side against the Patriots

CHAPTER ONE

∼

# The Consolidation of Slavery in the Mainland Colonies, 1619–1720

Throughout the sixteenth century, English thinking about how and where they might best exploit the economic opportunities presented by the Americas was heavily influenced by what they knew of Spanish, and to a lesser extent Portuguese, accomplishments in this part of the world. The stream of Spanish galleons laden down with gold and other precious metals that regularly made their way back to Europe testified to the enormous amount of wealth that the Americas offered both to governments and to private individuals. By way of contrast, British merchants and seamen, who were simultaneously exploiting the rich fishing banks off the North American coast and developing a trade in furs with Native Americans, were making pitiful amounts of money.

Beginning at Roanoke in the late 1580s, the English tried to emulate Spain and Portugal by establishing a permanent foothold in the North American mainland, a colony that would be their launching pad for money-making activities on a par with those of their Spanish and Portuguese rivals. The failure of Roanoke—the group of English men and women who had been left there had disappeared without a trace by 1590—did not deflect the English interest in colonization. By 1606 a group of English investors, who had organized themselves into the Virginia Company, were ready to unveil their blueprint for the colony, which they intended to found somewhere on the shoreline of Chesapeake Bay. They had also recruited a group of men who were willing to be sent as the first settlers of this new colony. However, these men, who included among their number artisans, soldiers, and an Anglican minister, as well as several gentlemen, did not seem particularly

1

well qualified for the kinds of heavy work involved in establishing a colony in the American wilderness. Yet as far as the Virginia Company was concerned, they were entirely adequate to undertake the money-making activities envisioned for this new settlement.

Nowhere in their plans for their colonizing venture did the Virginia Company make any mention of what, for the best part of a century, had been a well-known feature of many of the settlements established by Spain and Portugal in Latin America and the Caribbean: racially based systems of slavery that involved large numbers of both Native Americans and west and west central African peoples being forced into lifetime bondage. This omission did not reflect any deep-seated moral, religious, or philosophical opposition to the institution of slavery, or any particular concern for the rights of Native Americans and Africans, on the part of the men based in London who would administer the new colony of Virginia. It was simply the case that, for essentially practical reasons, their blueprint did not require anyone to be enslaved. Indeed, what they promised to those English people who they hoped would settle in Virginia was the exact opposite: freedom. What they meant by this was something that most people did not enjoy in the hierarchical society of early-seventeenth-century England: an economic freedom from dependence upon others.

Freedom in Virginia would be rooted in the ownership of land, something that was beyond the reach of most people in England. As time would quickly show, though, one major difficulty was that the vast amount of land granted to the Virginia Company by the English Crown was already occupied by native peoples who might be said to have had a moral, if not a legal, right to it. Unless it suited their purposes, these native peoples might not be willing partners in schemes hatched in London that threatened to deprive them of even the smallest amounts of that land.

The Virginia Company set out the three main ways in which it hoped to make money from its colony and, significantly, commercial agriculture was not one of them. First, and continuing in the vein of sixteenth-century thinking about the Americas, the Company believed that lucrative trading connections could be forged with native peoples, who would be keen to deal furs and skins for a variety of English manufactured goods. Second, following the Spanish example, but reflecting its ignorance of the local environment, the Company insisted that, with or without the help of the local inhabitants, gold and other precious metals would soon be discovered in Virginia. Third, they held out the hope that the waterways of the Chesapeake Bay region would lead the settlers to the Pacific Ocean and a money-making trade with the Orient. What the Virginia Company chose to ignore in its quest for quick returns on its investment was another model of development that was certainly known to it: the thriving sugar plantations that had been developed by Portugal and Spain in Brazil and the Caribbean. For the best part of a century, those plantations had been worked by people who had been forcibly removed from west and west central Africa in order to be enslaved in the Americas.

Within a matter of a few years, the Virginia Company's economic plan was in tatters. Settlers died in the hundreds from a range of unfamiliar diseases; at times they virtually starved to death; they quarreled among themselves; and periodically they fell out with the local Native American people and their leader, Powhatan. There was no gold or silver to be had; neither the Chesapeake Bay nor the James River seemed to be taking the settlers any closer to the Pacific Ocean; and few profits were being made from trading with Native Americans.

Despite these setbacks, the Virginia Company persisted and, through the 1610s, was still able to attract English settlers to their colony. But both the Company and those colonists who, against all the odds, had managed to survive realized that something had to be done if Virginia was ever to prosper. The Company introduced significant reforms, including, for the first time, the possibility of private land ownership. An important degree of self-government was provided in 1619 with the creation of the House of Burgesses. This was the first elected representative government anywhere in British America. Although the Virginia Company retained overall control of Virginia until 1625, the House of Burgesses gave the colonists a vital say in running their own affairs. For their part, by the mid-1610s, when all else seemed to have failed, the colonists turned to the plantation model that had been ignored by the Virginia Company back in 1606.

Environmentally, sugar could not be grown in the tidewater regions of the Chesapeake, but after some experimentation the settlers discovered that it was possible to grow tobacco, something that was in great and growing demand in Europe. In the mid-1610s the first shipment of tobacco was sent from Virginia to England and, from this point onward, that plant proved to be of fundamental significance in shaping virtually every aspect of life in this part of the southern mainland. Tobacco created entirely new demands for land and labor.

The commercial production of tobacco required large amounts of land and, by the 1620s, the Virginia settlers had no hesitation in using force to take what they needed from the Native American peoples who held it. In

1622 Jamestown had almost been wiped out by a Native American attack, and for the English survivors this was justification enough to use their superior military technology to grab the land they needed to expand their highly profitable tobacco-planting operations. This they would continue to do through the remainder of the seventeenth century.

If tobacco was to be produced on the scale envisioned by the colonists during the 1620s, then it required not only land but also more workers than could be supplied by Virginia's current English population. By the mid-1620s, that population numbered just over twelve hundred and it was nowhere near close to being able to reproduce itself naturally in sufficient numbers to satisfy the colony's swelling labor demands. The plantation model of Latin America and the Caribbean, which was well known to the English, offered a possible solution: enslaved workers. Yet this was not the solution turned to by Virginia's tobacco planters during the 1620s and 1630s, and the question is, why not? Why did they not turn to Africa, or more locally to Native Americans, for the workers they required?

We know that by the spring of 1619 there were already about thirty or forty west or west central African people in Virginia. How long they had been there, and precisely what status they had been given by the English, remains a mystery. Rather more famously, in the summer of the same year John Rolfe, the husband of the Native American princess Pocahontas, commented that a Dutch man of war had "sold" the Virginia settlers "twenty Negars." Quite coincidentally, or so it seems, this was precisely at the point when tobacco was beginning to generate enormous profits. However, there is no suggestion that either the colonists or the Virginia Company had arranged for the Dutch to supply these people. It seems that it was simply by chance that the Dutch had arrived at Port Comfort, where they had exchanged, or "sold," these "Negars" for the supplies they needed.

Given their labor requirements, and the money they were making from tobacco, it might have seemed logical for Virginia's tobacco planters to have seized upon the opportunity provided by the arrival of the Dutch man of war in 1619 and look to west and west central Africa for the workers they wanted. But they did not. African peoples remained demographically and economically insignificant in the Chesapeake until the last quarter of the seventeenth century. There were several reasons why this was so.

It was not that, during the first three-quarters of the seventeenth century, Virginia planters had such a deep-seated aversion to the institution of slavery that they made a positive choice to ignore the transatlantic slave trade as a source of agricultural workers. In fact, they had no choice in the matter. The

Virginia of the 1620s and 1630s held virtually no appeal to the Dutch shippers who dominated the transatlantic slave trade. Their chief, and guaranteed, markets lay further south, in the sugar-producing regions of Brazil and the Caribbean. To send vessels packed with valuable human cargoes to Virginia made little economic sense. Virginia's tobacco producers might have been making money, and well able to afford slaves, but their plantations were not numerous enough to absorb cargoes of up to two or three hundred people at a time. Moreover, despite the financial success of tobacco, Virginia was still a struggling, vulnerable colony. There was no assurance that a slave ship would find any customers waiting for it. Even if there were, tobacco plantations were strung out along the waters of Chesapeake Bay; there was no central, urban infrastructure to facilitate the speedy and efficient sale of enslaved people.

What happened in Barbados, which was first settled by the English in the late 1620s, suggests that it might well have been a very different story had African peoples actually been made available to Virginia's tobacco planters during the formative years of their tobacco economy. From the very beginning, commercial agriculture, initially in the shape of tobacco but by the late 1630s sugar, was the mainstay of an increasingly prosperous Barbadian economy. During the early 1640s the flow of English migrants to the island was disrupted by the civil war that was raging in England, but Barbadian sugar planters did not have to look far for an alternative source of labor.

Unlike Virginia, Barbados was directly on the route between west Africa, the Caribbean, and Latin America, and at no great trouble or cost to themselves, Dutch slave traders could easily provide the island's planters with as many enslaved workers as they wanted. Apparently without a second thought, or indeed without much thought at all, Barbadian sugar planters immediately took advantage of what the Dutch were offering them. By 1660, Barbados had a black majority, and there was no question at all but that this was an enslaved majority. As early as 1636, the royal governor and council of Barbados had decreed that any Africans already on the island would be considered enslaved, and by the early 1660s enslaved Africans were legally defined as pieces of property. Had Virginia been in the same situation as Barbados, its planters may well have followed a similar path during the tobacco boom years of the 1620s and 1630s.

Of course, Virginia planters had an option open to them that was denied their English counterparts in Barbados: an indigenous population. By the time the English set about colonizing Barbados there was no sign of an Amerindian population that might have been exploited as a workforce. Theoretically, Virginia's tobacco producers could have secured all the workers they needed from the local Native American population, whose lands they were busy snatching in order to expand their planting operations. In fact, they never saw Native Americans as being the ideal way of satisfying their labor needs. Later on, the English who settled in other parts of the North American mainland would enslave some Native Americans. However, this would be on a very small scale indeed, except in South Carolina, where Native Americans made up around a quarter of that colony's enslaved workforce by the first decade of the eighteenth century.

Initially the Virginia Company had declared its intent to trade with the indigenous populations of the Chesapeake and also expressed its wish to convert as many of them as possible to Protestant Christianity. These two purposes prompted the development of an extremely positive, but in many ways an entirely self-serving, English stereotype of Native Americans. To declare that Native Americans were capable of being converted to Christianity, that they had souls, was an implicit acknowledgment of their humanity, if not of their complete equality with those of European descent. The supposed willingness of Native Americans to exchange, or sell, their furs and pelts to English traders in return for English woolens and metal goods led to them being depicted as cooperative and ever-helpful trading partners. In other words, the English constructed an idealized image of the Native American that was not only best suited but was also absolutely essential to the successful implementation of their plans for the North American mainland.

Yet as there had been for most of the sixteenth century, there was another, far more negative, aspect to the way in which they stereotyped Native Americans. Could these people, who heavily outnumbered the first colonists, actually be trusted? What part might they have played in the disappearance of the English who had settled at Roanoke? Especially after the attack on Jamestown in 1622, in which almost 350 settlers had been killed, this negative image came increasingly to the fore, and Native Americans were depicted as dangerous and violent enemies.

Both the positive and the negative aspects of the stereotype constructed by the English diminished the attractiveness of Native Americans as a potential labor force for Virginia's expanding tobacco economy. It did not make good business sense to enslave one's trading partners, especially given their numerical superiority and their capacity to retaliate. Even if Native Americans captured in war, or by raiding parties, were put to work in the tobacco fields, there was nothing to prevent their escape. Moreover, Native Americans, especially men, had an appalling stereotype as workers. Excellent hunters and fishermen they might be, but agricultural workers they were not. In addition to stereotyping Native Americans as untrustworthy and dangerous, the English often dismissed them as being far too lazy to make productive farm hands. In their societies, or so it seemed to the English, women did most of the hard agricultural labor. From the perspective of Virginia's tobacco planters, there was absolutely no reason to turn to Native Americans for the labor they needed. It made far more sense to wage war upon them, to slaughter them, and to forcibly seize that which the English really wanted from them, their lands.

Virginia tobacco planters were seeking efficient and trustworthy agricultural workers, as well as men who could be called upon to defend their interests against attacks launched against them by either Native Americans or Britain's continental European rivals. Between the 1620s and the last quarter of the seventeenth century they looked across the Atlantic for those workers–not to west and west central Africa, but to Britain.

Before its collapse in the mid-1620s, the Virginia Company had produced a steady flow of pamphlets and other publications designed to attract investment capital and settlers for its colony. Needless to say, this literature did not mention the death and disease, the fragile relations with Native Americans, and the other hardships of life in early Virginia. Instead, it suggested that here was a well-nigh perfect physical environment, a land where individuals could make a handsome living without having to engage in hard physical labor, and a land where they could quickly become their own masters rather than being dependent upon others for their livelihood.

As with many human migrations, that to Virginia during the seventeenth century was a mixture of "push" and "pull." British men, and by the 1620s British women, were being promised an infinitely better life in Virginia than they could ever hope to enjoy if they remained in Britain. Social and economic ambition combined with social and economic hardship and desperation persuaded thousands of people to cross the Atlantic to take their chances in Virginia.

The difficulty for most of these potential migrants was that they simply could not afford to pay the cost of their passage to the new life that awaited them on the other side of the Atlantic. The solution arrived at by the 1620s was a variation on the contractual forms of employment that were commonplace in Britain. Under what became known as indentured servitude, migrants agreed to work for an employer in Virginia, usually for around five or six years, in exchange for their passage to the colony. Once there, they would be fed and clothed by their master or mistress and, once they had completed their term of service, would be given their freedom. They might also expect to receive a few goods, such as tools, or a small cash payment to help them on their way. All the conditions of the service were set out in a legally binding contract. Indentured servitude, then, was regarded as a stepping-stone along the path to economic freedom and socioeconomic advancement.

Until the 1670s and 1680s, the willingness of English people to emigrate to the Chesapeake as indentured servants dovetailed perfectly with the labor needs of that region's tobacco producers. Between the 1620s and about 1680, around 80 percent of all the British people who emigrated to the Chesapeake did so as indentured servants. They were generally a young population and largely composed of men, who outnumbered women by as many as five or six to one. Once in America they were put to work in the tobacco fields and those who did not work hard enough to satisfy their masters and mistresses could be subjected to harsh physical punishment. However, if they survived their term of indenture they could look forward to legal and economic freedom and a high proportion went on to become land owners and tobacco producers in their own right through the mid-seventeenth century.

Although tobacco planters depended heavily upon indentured servants, some Africans were also brought to the Chesapeake, not as a direct result of the transatlantic slave trade but as a consequence of the trading links that had been forged between the British Caribbean islands and the North American mainland. Their numbers, though, were very small. In 1625, for instance, there were only twenty-three people of African descent in Virginia. A quarter of a century later, when Virginia's total population had climbed to 15,300, there were still only about 300 Africans in the colony. By 1660, the roughly 950 people of African ancestry accounted for between 3 and 4 percent of Virginia's population. These people were put to work in the tobacco fields. They often labored alongside indentured servants and sometimes their masters. It seems that black and white workers socialized with each other after their day's work; sometimes they ran away together. Unfortunately, we have no firsthand accounts from these people about just how important differences of race and ethnicity were to them.

One thing that can be said with certainty is that this small African component of the Virginia population was not immediately enslaved by the English. In fact, their legal status remained somewhat ambiguous until the late seventeenth century. Some Africans might have been given contracts similar to indentured servants, and this could have been true of a man named Anthony Johnson, who went on to become a land owner and the master of other Africans. However, despite these ambiguities, it is evident that beginning in 1619, when John Rolfe used the term Negars instead of servants, or African servants, people of west and west central African ancestry were conceived of and in various ways treated as a group separate from and inferior to the English.

The English sense of their own superiority and of African inferiority did not suddenly spring up in Virginia and Barbados in the 1620s. Many of the travel accounts written during the sixteenth century by English men who had visited west and west central Africa depicted the inhabitants of these regions as barely human. They were accused of cannibalism, of having sex with animals, and being more like apes than men and women. If, as the English believed, all humanity was descended from Adam and Eve, who they assumed must have had white skins, did this mean that black-skinned Africans were not human? If, as some argued, black-skinned Africans were human, then they were descended from Ham, the son of Noah, who had been cursed by God for witnessing his father's nakedness. Since the English commonly associated the color black with sin, it was all too easy to arrive at the conclusion that God had decreed perpetual bondage as part of the Africans' punishment.

This negative, and damning, stereotyping of African peoples could be used to justify their enslavement in British America, but it was neither the initial nor the sole cause of their enslavement. Enslavement occurred only when the use of slaves, rather than indentured servants, became economically rational and viable. In the case of Virginia, this would not become the case until the last quarter of the seventeenth century. Yet the fact remains that, from the 1620s, several elements of what would eventually become that colony's slave society were slowly but surely being put in place. The small number of Africans in early Virginia did not represent, and neither were they regarded as being, a serious threat to the interests of the colony's British inhabitants. Africans were without a power base, and they lacked allies, both in Virginia and in Britain, who might help them to protect their interests. If, as happened in 1640 to an African man named John Punch who had run away from his master in the company of two European-born servants, a Virginia court decided that it was acceptable for an African to be made to work for life, one of the fundamental components of enslavement, then there was no way of appealing that decision.

Nor was there any way in which, as was beginning to happen by the 1630s, planters could be stopped from placing a higher valuation on African women workers than they did on indentured European women. African women could be made to perform hard agricultural labor, which many European women found unacceptable, and their children forced to follow in their footsteps. Here we see, by the 1630s and 1640s, albeit in a shadowy form, the beginnings of a second attribute of slavery, the legal status of a child being determined by that of its mother.

By the middle of the seventeenth century, the Virginia law courts were beginning to deny the very humanity of Africans when they declared that a master could not be found guilty of murdering an African servant because who would be so foolish as to destroy his own property? A few years later, the Africans' last hopes of avoiding enslavement on a significant scale were dashed when the Virginia government concluded that religion made no difference to their legal status. Not surprisingly, Virginia's planter-politicians answered the age-old question of whether one Christian could hold another Christian in perpetual bondage in a way that best suited their economic self-interest. There was nothing to stop those Africans who chose to convert to Christianity, but they were deluding themselves if they thought that this would make any difference to their worldly status. Virginia's labor-hungry tobacco planters were desperate to secure a permanent and, if at all possible, a self-perpetuating workforce and there was virtually nothing that the colony's still comparatively small black population could do to prevent them.

It would be a combination of factors, in Britain and in the Chesapeake, which signaled the beginning of the transformation of Virginia's labor force from a heavy dependence upon indentured whites to an equally heavy dependence upon enslaved black workers by the 1670s and 1680s. Among other things, declining mortality rates meant that more servants were surviving their term of indenture and entering into competition with their former employers in what was now an economically depressed tobacco market. Social, economic, and political tensions erupted in 1676 in the shape of Bacon's Rebellion. In what was virtually a civil war in Virginia, an eminent planter named Nathaniel Bacon assumed the leadership of these discontented people who took up arms against those who remained loyal to the British-appointed governor, Sir William Berkeley. Bacon's Rebellion ended with Bacon's death—from natural causes—in the fall of 1676. Nathaniel Bacon had not openly questioned the treatment of blacks in Virginia, but as far as many eminent tobacco planters were concerned, one of the most worrying aspects of the movement he had led was that armed blacks had fought alongside whites. This raised the horrifying prospect of a dangerous alliance. Blacks and underclass whites seemed to be cooperating in a way that emphasized shared economic grievances and minimized racial and ethnic differences. If this was not bad enough for tobacco planters, an upturn in the

English economy was lessening the number of migrants to North America. The settling of new colonies, such as Pennsylvania, during the second half of the seventeenth century heightened the competition for the fewer number of British people who were now willing to cross to North America as indentured servants. Virginia tobacco planters could no longer depend upon securing the workers they needed from Britain.

Yet something else was happening in England that would ensure that the Chesapeake's tobacco planters were supplied with the workers they required. The 1660s and 1670s witnessed a heightened interest on the part of the English in commerce and colonization, and integral to this was a growing English involvement in the transatlantic slave trade. Merchants who had made healthy profits by transporting indentured servants to the plantation colonies were set to make even more money by entering the slave trade. By the 1680s, Virginia's tobacco planters were more than willing to do business with them in order to obtain the labor they required.

There was no ambiguity whatsoever about the legal status of the thousands of African people who now began to flood into the Chesapeake. Between 1700 and 1740, for example, approximately 49,000 Africans were imported into Virginia and Maryland. In the late 1680s Africans had accounted for around 11 percent of the Virginia population; by 1740 they accounted for around 40 percent. Simultaneously, Virginia and Maryland were being transformed from societies with slaves into slave societies, and a racially based system of slavery would shape and dominate virtually every aspect of life. Beginning in the late seventeenth century, an attempt to impose racial control, in order to generate as well as to safeguard profits, quickly became one of the top priorities of the Chesapeake's leading tobacco producers. There was nothing haphazard or ill-thought-out about their strategy.

In 1705 Virginia's planter-dominated House of Burgesses drew up a code of laws that sought to do three main things: to confirm the perpetual and inherited bondage of people of African descent; to establish an entirely separate penal code and judicial system for enslaved people; and, finally, through such devices as compulsory service in slave patrols, to compel nonslaveholders to protect the property rights of those who did. In part, this latter provision was also designed to try to drive a wedge between the colony's black and white workforce. The planter effort to emphasize racial difference at the expense of class solidarity was also evident in the language used by Virginia's lawmakers to explain and to justify why this slave code was necessary. This was a language steeped in racial abuse, seeking to degrade men and women of African descent and virtually denying them their humanity.

Seventeenth-century Virginia provided English colonists with one model of enslaving African peoples but there were others. For example, further south, the English colony of South Carolina imported wholesale the Barbadian slave system during the 1660s. The small size of Barbados limited the possibilities for the further expansion of sugar cultivation, and planters were keen to expand their planting operations to the North American mainland. Their ambitions fitted neatly with those of the eminent Englishmen who in 1663 secured a charter from the English Crown authorizing them to settle a new colony to the south of Virginia. Barbadian planters, however, were unwilling to move to Carolina, unless they received cast-iron guarantees that they would continue to enjoy the right to use slaves, and these they received in 1669. Virtually from the beginning, a racially based system of slavery was legally sanctioned in South Carolina.

It was not until the 1720s and 1730s that rice emerged as the main export crop in the South Carolina lowcountry, but even before that the colony's planters were heavily dependent upon enslaved African workers. The number of enslaved people imported into the colony each year, almost exclusively through the port of Charleston, ranged from just over 400 in 1725 to about 3,000 in 1736. South Carolina's enslaved population grew from around 4,000 in 1708 to just over 39,000 in 1740. In 1708 South Carolina was already half black; within a few years it would be two-thirds black, and the only mainland colony with a black majority.

A very different model emerged in New England. The possibility that slavery might exist in Massachusetts had been acknowledged as early as 1641, within ten years of the colony's first settlement. John Winthrop and the other Puritan founders of Massachusetts set sail for North America with the intention of establishing God's kingdom upon earth. For every aspect of life in their Godly society they looked for guidance to the Bible, and particularly to the Old Testament. The Old Testament provided them with what they regarded as a wholly legitimate, and quite distinctive, set of circumstances under which slavery could exist in their society. These were set out in the Body of Liberties, which was drawn up in 1641. This document was rather like a constitution. It set out the rights to be enjoyed by the settlers as well as regulations that were intended to govern virtually every aspect of their lives.

According to the Body of Liberties, there were three main ways in which a person might be legitimately enslaved. First, and in keeping with long-standing English and continental European thought, this could happen if someone was taken prisoner in a just war, which usually meant a war fought by Christians against non-Christians. Second, it was possible to be sold into slavery and, third, to sell oneself into slavery. The Body of Liberties went on to describe the ways in which those held as slaves should be treated and, based upon Old Testament distinctions between Jewish and non-Jewish servants, the result was something of a halfway house. On the one hand, the slave was to be considered as the property of his or her owner but, on the other hand, the slave was also legally defined as a person who enjoyed certain rights. These rights included the right to hold property and, significantly, to sue and to be sued in the courts.

The Body of Liberties made no mention of the race or ethnicity of potential slaves but it was one that could readily and conveniently be applied to Native Americans. During the mid-1630s, war had broken out between the colonists and the Pequot people—mainly over land—and the question became what to do with those Native Americans who had been taken captive. The Puritans had no great wish to keep them in their midst, let alone return them, so instead they shipped them to the Caribbean where they were probably exchanged for Africans who were shipped back to Massachusetts. In any event, the first Africans are known to have arrived in Massachusetts in the late 1630s and, thereafter, the peculiar Puritan concept of bondage was reserved for them.

Given the different labor needs of New England's small family farms compared to those of the plantation colonies, relatively few African people were taken to that region. By 1660, for example, New England's population numbered around 33,000 people, of whom only 560 were of African descent. Put another way, there were about as many Africans in the whole of New England as might be found in a single slave ship heading for Barbados. Fifty years later there were still only around 1,900 Africans in New England, and they accounted for barely 2 percent of the region's population.

The English colonists introduced black slavery to Virginia and New England, and brought it with them from Barbados to South Carolina. In the 1660s, when they captured the Dutch colony of New Netherland, which they renamed New York, they inherited a system of slavery that dated back to the 1620s and 1630s. That system continued, only now under English law. In practice, the English takeover made little difference to black slaves. They still worked as agricultural laborers and filled various skilled and unskilled jobs in the port town of New York.

During the 1670s the sparsely settled southern portion of the territory taken from the Dutch attracted the attention of a group of English people who, for a mixture of religious and economic reasons, were keen to establish a colony of their own in America. Rather like the Puritans fifty years earlier, the Quakers thought that America offered them not only a way of escaping religious persecution in England but also an opportunity to create their ideal society. In the late 1670s the Quakers were allowed to settle in the area that became known as New Jersey. A few years later, in 1681, they were given permission by the English crown to establish another colony to the south of New York. This new settlement would be named Pennsylvania in recognition of the Quaker leader, William Penn.

William Penn described his plans for Pennsylvania as a "Holy Experiment." Freedom of religious worship was guaranteed to all the settlers, but steps were taken to ensure that the Quakers would control Pennsylvania's government. Penn was determined to establish a secure sanctuary for Quakers, but he and his coreligionists were also keen to make money out of this new venture. Generous land grants were offered to prospective migrants, and choice locations in the colony's capital, Philadelphia, were given to those of them who had capital to invest. Because of this mixture of religious freedom and the prospect of economic gain, Penn was extremely successful in attracting British and European migrants to Pennsylvania. During the 1690s around 10,000 people settled in the colony, and their growing prosperity depended in part upon the use of black slaves.

During the mid-eighteenth century, the Quakers became the most vocal critics of slavery and the transatlantic slave trade. However, to begin with, William Penn had no objections to the enslavement of Africans. His position, and that of most other Quakers, was that slavery was perfectly acceptable, provided that slave owners attended to the spiritual and material needs of those they enslaved. As long as this was done, there was no scriptural reason why Christians should not hold people, including other Christians, as slaves. Given this reassurance, many Quakers soon became slaveholders. It has been estimated that as early as 1700 about 10 percent of the families in Philadelphia owned at least one slave. Much of Philadelphia's prosperity came from trade, and very soon the city's merchants, including many prominent Quaker merchants, were involved in the transatlantic slave trade. Some of the slaves they imported were for the local market, but most were destined for the plantation colonies of the southern mainland and the British Caribbean.

By the late seventeenth century, everywhere in the North American mainland, the English colonists had devised systems of perpetual bondage that linked an individual's legal status to his or her skin color. Yet this formulation did not always work. It was possible to have a black complexion and to be legally free. In some cases this resulted from the right of owners to do what they wanted with their human property. If they wished, they could free their slaves either during their lifetime or after their death. Governments, too, offered freedom to slaves who risked their lives by fighting in various colonial wars or who were willing to betray slave conspiracies. However it happened, though, the granting of freedom was an extremely rare occurrence. At the end of the seventeenth century, free blacks comprised a minuscule proportion of the slave population of every mainland colony, and this situation did not change dramatically before the era of the American Revolution.

The English colonists had taken somewhat dissimilar routes to arrive at the conclusion that slavery was an appropriate legal status for those with black skin, but for most of the African men and women they sought to exploit, and to place in perpetual bondage, there had been only one route to their enslavement in British America, and that was via the transatlantic slave trade.

# CHAPTER TWO

# The Transatlantic Slave Trade

By the time the English first settled at Jamestown in 1607, the transatlantic slave trade had been in operation for a century or so. That trade sought to satisfy what seemed to be the insatiable demand of Portuguese settlers in Brazil, and their Spanish counterparts in the Caribbean, for slaves to work the sugar plantations that they had established there during the course of the sixteenth century. The main reason why this planter demand for enslaved labor remained so high was because of the appallingly high mortality rates experienced among slaves. Reflecting the harsh and often hazardous work involved in growing and refining sugar, the life expectancy of a newly arrived African slaves in these sugar colonies could be as little as seven years.

Given the enormous profits sugar planters were making from what came to be known as "white gold," which stemmed from the ravenous European appetite for their product, they could easily afford to replenish their workers. They regarded those workers as being little more than disposable commodities, or animals that, like their mules and horses, could be quite easily replaced.

Vast profits were made from sugar, and precisely the same was true when it came to supplying the labor that was believed essential to the production of that commodity. From the early sixteenth century onward, and without taking any noticeable interest in the morality of slave trading, European merchants and ships' captains, including English merchants and captains, desperately sought a piece of the action. Mainly because of deteriorating Anglo-Spanish relations, which stemmed from intense rivalry in both Europe and the Americas, the English were denied commercial access to the Spanish American colonies. Instead, the Spanish, as well as the Portuguese, looked to Dutch merchants to supply them with their slaves. Those merchants continued to dominate the transatlantic slave trade through the middle years of the following century.

As long as their labor needs were being satisfied by British migrants, the question of who controlled the transatlantic slave trade was of no real consequence to the tobacco growers of Virginia and Maryland. By the same token, the Chesapeake was of little interest to Dutch slave traders. It only became of interest to slave traders when the tobacco economy became sufficiently established to absorb human cargoes of up to three or four hundred people at a time. During the last third of the seventeenth century, it would be the British, rather than the Dutch, who stepped in to supply those cargoes.

Britain and its great commercial rival Holland went to war in the mid-seventeenth century. As a consequence of the British victory, New Netherland, soon to be renamed New York and already a slave-holding society, was added to Britain's expanding North American empire. The war also eliminated the Dutch as major trading rivals in British America and paved the way for British and colonial merchants to enter the transatlantic slave trade on a significant scale.

The first sign of British intention to monopolize the supply of enslaved Africans to its American colonies came in 1672, with the formation of The Royal African Company, which was given the sole right to deliver slaves to every part of British America. It continued to enjoy this monopoly through the early years of the eighteenth century. Thereafter, growing numbers of colonial merchants based in such port towns as Newport, Boston, New York, Philadelphia, and Charleston began to participate in the burgeoning transatlantic slave trade. Individual fortunes, as well as the growing prosperity of these urban economies and their surrounding areas, owed a great deal to the profits that were made from this trade in human flesh.

Between the late seventeenth and the mid-eighteenth centuries, the British sugar islands remained the main markets for British and colonial slave traders. However, beginning in the 1680s the demand for slaves also started to grow in the tobacco-producing areas of the tidewater Chesapeake, as it did in South Carolina during the 1720s and 1730s as rice became that colony's major export. For different lengths of time, the enslaved populations of the Chesapeake and South Carolina failed to reproduce themselves naturally in sufficient numbers to satisfy the continuing labor demands of tobacco and rice planters. This was mainly because of the imbalanced sex-ratios of the Africans imported into the Southern colonies.

By the 1750s and 1760s, natural reproduction was largely satisfying the labor needs of Virginia and Maryland planters, but this was still not the case

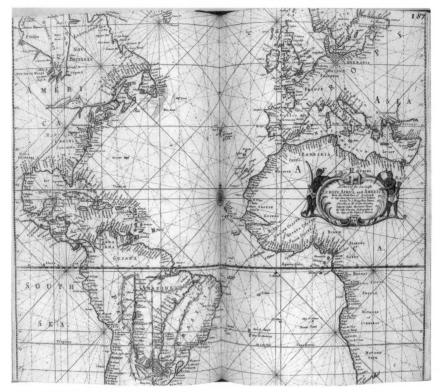

**Mariners' Chart of the Atlantic Ocean**

*Source:* John Seller, *The English Pilot. The Fourth Book* (London, 1689). By permission of the Syndics of Cambridge University Library.

further south. Rice cultivation was expanding, and by 1750 indigo, a dye that was in heavy demand by the British textile industry, was added to the lowcountry's exports. More slave workers were required than were being born to the enslaved people already in that region. On the eve of the war for American Independence, South Carolina and Georgia planters still depended on the transatlantic slave trade for the workers they needed. This was an important difference between the two plantation regions of the southern mainland, and it would be reflected in the positions they adopted during the nationwide debates about the future of the slave trade that took place during the era of the American Revolution.

Family formation was taking place within the enslaved populations of the southern colonies by the late seventeenth century. Children were being born to enslaved parents, but the phenomenal growth in the size of those populations during the next seventy-five years was almost entirely due to the transatlantic slave trade. Tobacco and rice planters alike turned eagerly to that trade. To say the least, Thomas Jefferson's assertion in the Declaration of Independence that the transatlantic slave trade had been forced upon reluctant American colonists by a tyrannical British Crown bears little truth to the reality of the situation. The profit motives of British and colonial merchants and southern planters dovetailed perfectly.

The sheer pace and scale of the transformation of the labor regimes of the southern mainland from a dependence upon indentured servants to enslaved Africans as a direct result of the transatlantic slave trade is immediately evident from the numbers of African peoples who were forcibly transported there after the 1680s. Before the closing of the transatlantic slave trade in the early nineteenth century, somewhere between 600,000 and 650,000 Africans were taken to the mainland, mostly to the southern mainland. But numbers alone reveal only a part, albeit an important part, of the continuing story of the evolution of slavery and race relations in that region. In themselves, they can do no more than hint at the extent of the human suffering, as well as the human resilience, which was an enduring characteristic of the transatlantic slave trade.

Many different aspects of the lives of the literally thousands of African peoples who survived the Middle Passage to North America were determined not only by their number and dispersal once in the Americas but also by their African origins. These ethnic origins varied both regionally and over time, but there were some broad patterns that would make possible both the survival and the blending of their different cultural backgrounds and experiences. Between 1720 and 1740, for example, Virginia acquired slaves mainly from the Bight of Benin and the Bight of Biafra or Angola. During the 1730s, Angola, and to a much lesser extent the Gambia, were the main sources of women and men who were imported into South Carolina.

In part, these import patterns, which could mean that newly arrived Africans stood a good chance of encountering their fellow countrymen and women once in America, reflected the ethnic preferences of tobacco and rice planters. By the 1730s and 1740s, based on their experience, planters were attaching certain attributes, such as work habits, to the African peoples and replenished their workforces accordingly. For example, the people taken from Gambia and Angola were widely thought of as being good workers, while according to some white commentators, the Ibo (Ebo) were believed to be highly emotional and suicide prone.

The British and colonial merchants and ships' captains who were involved in the transatlantic slave trade were well aware of these preferences, but they did not directly control who was and who was not presented to them as candidates for captivity in America. Neither did they reject those who enjoyed an unfavorable reputation in the eyes of colonial planters. Their main concern was with making a profit, and that meant packing their ships with whomever they could get hold of.

There were various circumstances in which African peoples found themselves being made available, often by African middle men, to British and colonial slave traders. Sometimes it was because they had been taken as prisoners of war or been kidnapped; others were gotten rid of by their rulers because they were seen as a dangerous political or religious threat to the status quo; and, if European commentators are to be believed, there were even those who had been sold into slavery by their families.

Wherever they originally came from, and regardless of the way in which they had first been taken into captivity, there were some important similarities in the experiences of those who found themselves in the hands of transatlantic slave traders. For most people, young and old, men, women, and children alike, the first stage of what would be their truly appalling journey to British America began with being forced to walk chained together, often for hundreds of miles, to one or another of the slaving forts that had been established by the European powers at various points along the west African coast. How long they remained at forts such as Goree, where they were often kept penned up, varied from a few hours to a few weeks, depending upon how many of them had been assembled there and whether or not a slave ship was ready and waiting to take them on board. As an unmistakable sign that they were now considered not so much as human beings but as a form of property, many Africans were branded with a red-hot iron before being loaded on to the slave ships.

It is difficult to imagine the shock, the horror, and the sheer uncertainty of those who were taken to the slave forts. The question to which they had no clear answer was what would happen to them next. Why were they being taken on board these ships by these white people? Needless to say, virtually none of those who had previously been taken into captivity by Europeans had returned to tell their stories. Rumors abounded, of which one of the most common was that Europeans were cannibals, and that Africans would be taken, dead or alive, to some far-off place, where they would be eaten. What for many Africans must have been the utter relief of not being killed, as soon as they set foot on board the slave ships, must have been very quickly

**Slave "Forts" on the West African Coast**

*Source:* William Bosman, *A New and Accurate Description of the Coast of Guinea* (London, 1794). By permission of the Syndics of Cambridge University Library.

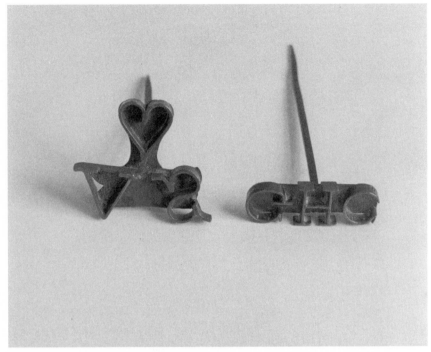

**Branding Irons with Owners' Initials**
*Source:* The Bridgman Art Library. By permission of Wilberforce House, Hull City Museums and Art Galleries.

replaced by total horror at the dreadfulness of the conditions that awaited them on board those vessels.

Some captains and surgeons serving on the slave ships left written reports of conditions on board. However, there is only one detailed account of the journey to British America, or the Middle Passage as it was often known, prior to the American Revolution that was produced by an African slave. Olaudah Equiano, sometimes known by the European name of Gustavus Vassa, had been forced to travel in the holds of one of these ships as a young child. In the late eighteenth century, several years after he had managed to secure his freedom from slavery, Equiano published his autobiography. His graphic description of the atrocious conditions on board the slave ship to America would have been entirely familiar to the thousands upon thousands of men, women, and children who found themselves in precisely the same situation as he did. If these men, women, and children lived to tell their tales, and thousands of them did not, then in pre-Revolutionary America they would be tales that they told to their offspring. The telling and retelling of these stories, and the memories of Africa they evoked, became a central feature of the folk culture that evolved in the slave quarters of the American South.

From the time African men and women, of all ages and backgrounds, first set foot on board the slave ships, their experiences were both similar and

**Olaudah Equiano**

Source: Olaudah Equiano, *The Interesting Narrative of the Life of Olaudah Equiano, or Gustavus Vassa, The African: Written by Himself* (London, 1789). By permission of the Syndics of Cambridge University Library.

dissimilar. The records kept by Europeans involved in the slave trade suggest that on many, probably most, slave ships, men heavily outnumbered women, sometimes by around six or seven to one. Most ships' captains knew only too well that their human cargoes would do everything in their power to avoid whatever fate it was that awaited them, and that their best hope of making good their escape was while the African coast remained in sight and within reach. But they associated this, and other forms of violent physical resistance, with men, not with women. What many captains failed to realize was that the usually smaller number of women on board their ships did not always passively accept whatever the future might hold in store for them.

One expression of these perceptions of the resistance they might encounter from African men and women, and something that actually enabled women and men to cooperate in offering whatever opposition they could to their oppressors, was in the way in which many ships' captains packed their human cargoes. On most vessels, men were chained together, often in pairs, and crammed below deck in the ship's holds. Often they were wedged together so tightly that they barely had enough space to turn over, and the dimensions of the hold were such that it was difficult for them to be able to stand up straight. Holds were usually windowless and they very quickly became stifling. Sanitation facilities were primitive in the extreme. The men were forced to relieve themselves in tubs or buckets, which were often left uncovered and irregularly emptied. In order to reach these tubs and buckets, they were forced to clamber over and to step upon one another. As Equiano reported, the stench in the holds of the slave ships was unimaginable and simply overpowering.

Usually, these were the appalling conditions that men experienced for twenty-two or twenty-three hours a day for a minimum of five or six weeks, the time it took to cross the Atlantic. They might be brought up to the top deck, still chained together, once or twice a day where they were fed and sometimes washed by being hosed down. In the event of bad weather, however, they remained in the holds for days on end.

It is scarcely surprising that conditions like these produced a range of diseases and infections in the holds of many slave ships. Diarrhea and dysentery were commonplace, as were a range of infectious sores and ulcers. Ships' surgeons did what they could, but the remedies available to them were often totally ineffective. Slaves who died were unceremoniously thrown overboard and sometimes, in order to prevent the further spread of sickness among the valuable human cargo, those who showed the signs of a deadly disease were tossed into the sea while they were still alive. The demand for slaves, espe-

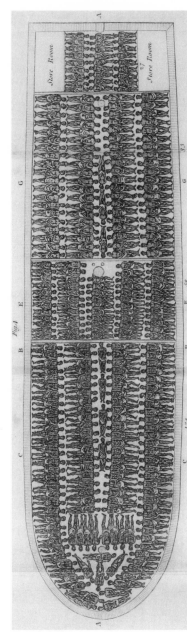

**The Way in which a Slave Ship Was Loaded**

*Source:* Thomas Clarkson, *The History of the Rise, Progress, and Accomplishment of the Abolition of the African Slave-Trade by the British Parliament* (London, 1808). By permission of the Syndics of Cambridge University Library.

cially in the plantation colonies, remained so great that even with mortality rates that ranged from 5 to 20 percent, most voyages were profitable and some were highly so.

On some slave ships women and children were also placed in the holds, but it seems to have been more usual for them to have been put between decks. Sometimes, like men, they were chained together, sometimes they were not. Generally speaking, they were not thought to pose any great risk to the physical safety of the ships' white crew members. Women might have had more personal space, and were allowed a relatively greater degree of movement, than men, but this could come at a great cost. They were not immune to any disease on board the vessel and they were also vulnerable to sexual exploitation by the ship's captain and crew. On some ships, captains tried to prevent such exploitation; on others they did not.

Given the conditions on board slave ships, and the awesome amount of firepower available to their white crews, the possibility of serious slave resistance might seem very remote indeed. In fact, the reverse was true. These human cargoes summoned the will, and found the means, to resist their captivity in ways that shocked, but also occasionally earned the admiration of, their captors.

Slave resistance on board the ships was of two kinds. First, there was armed resistance, sometimes reflecting a cooperative effort on the part of men and women. This might be facilitated by the white crew's oversight, neglect, or overconfidence. For example, on one slaver the men were brought up from the holds to be fed and were given knives with which to cut their food. It was only with difficulty that the white crew was able to ward off the assault that followed. Sometimes, women were able to obtain knives and other weapons, which they managed to smuggle to the men in the holds. On some ships, these men were able to hold off the attempts made by the white crew to disarm and overpower them for many hours.

We will never know for certain exactly how many uprisings took place on the slave ships heading to the mainland colonies prior to the American Revolution, but there were certainly enough to put ships' captains and crews on their guard, and many slave ships were like floating fortresses. Their superior weaponry meant that it was virtually certain that sooner or later they would be able to crush any insurrection taking place on board their vessels. When they did so, they usually wreaked their vengeance on any survivors, particularly those known or thought to have been the ringleaders. Their fate, which was also intended to act as a deterrent to those of their compatriots who were often made to watch the event, was usually to be hanged alive from the ship's yardarm. Others might be whipped to within an inch of their lives.

The second form of resistance offered on board slave ships was suicide, which often perplexed white crew members. Some women and men starved themselves to death, often despite severe floggings and the crude efforts that were made to force-feed them. On other occasions, they threw themselves into the sea and resisted any and all attempts to rescue them. What puzzled many white crew members was not the despair but the unadulterated happiness with which these people met their deaths. In keeping with a widespread African belief, they were firmly convinced that after death their souls, or spirits, would return home. This belief persisted for many decades in the enslaved communities of the Americas. Much to the consternation of their colonial owners, some enslaved people killed themselves soon after their arrival in America.

The next ordeal for those who had managed or chosen to survive the Middle Passage began with their arrival in the port towns of the mainland colonies. Here their immediate fates and prospects were determined as they were disposed of to their new colonial owners. In every port town, the usual method of selling new arrivals was by public auction, which occurred sometimes in taverns, in merchant houses, or in the open air. Depending upon the method favored by the local merchant or merchants to whom these women and men had been originally consigned, this could mean being offered for sale either alone or as part of a group. At this point any links of family and friendship that somehow or other had survived, or been forged on, the Middle Passage might be forever broken.

For obvious financial reasons, planters and others who attended slave auctions were concerned with the health and physical fitness as well as with the ages and African origins of the men and women offered for sale. The prices they were willing to pay for slaves reflected these concerns. Young, fit slaves who could be made to work at hard agricultural labor were in the greatest demand, and they fetched the highest prices. Newly arrived slaves might find themselves standing on the auction block, either naked or with a minimum of clothing, while their prospective buyers poked and prodded and subjected them to the most detailed and embarrassing physical examination. Such scenes would be repeated time and time again in towns and cities of the mainland colonies, as owners bought and sold enslaved people.

Depending upon where their new owner lived, the final leg of the journey from Africa could range from a few yards to several miles. A minority of newly arrived Africans were purchased by local buyers and remained in or

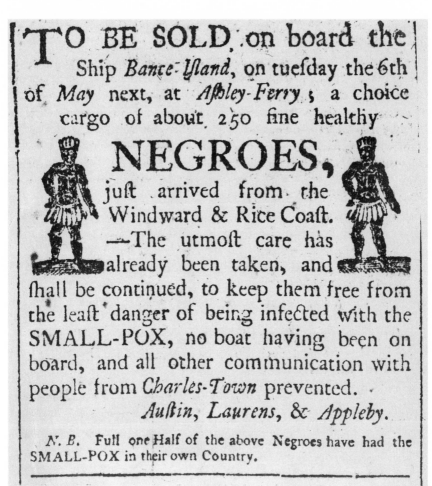

**TO BE SOLD** on board the Ship *Bance-Island*, on tuefday the 6th of *May* next, at *Afhley-Ferry* ; a choice cargo of about 250 fine healthy

# NEGROES,

juft arrived from the Windward & Rice Coaft. —The utmoft care has already been taken, and fhall be continued, to keep them free from the leaft danger of being infected with the SMALL-POX, no boat having been on board, and all other communication with people from *Charles-Town* prevented.

*Auftin, Laurens, & Appleby.*

N. B. Full one Half of the above Negroes have had the SMALL-POX in their own Country.

**Newspaper Advertisement Announcing the Sale of Slaves in Charleston, South Carolina**
*Source: South Carolina Gazette* (circa 1775). By permission of the Library of Congress.

close to the port towns to which they had been delivered. The vast majority found themselves being removed from those towns to the countryside. Beginning in the late seventeenth century onward, several of those women and men who were taken to the tobacco and rice plantations of the southern mainland had to face yet another ordeal once they reached their new home. If they had not been branded before leaving Africa, then there was a good chance that it would happen to them upon their arrival in America.

In early modern Britain and continental Europe, branding with a red-hot iron was used as method of punishing criminals. In the mainland American colonies, and more particularly in the southern plantation colonies, it was employed with a rather different purpose. The use of the branding iron was making an unmistakable statement of the slave owners, who asserted complete possession by disfiguring the body. It was an explicit attempt to deny the humanity of people of African origin. Women and men were branded on the chest, the shoulder, or cheek; sometimes, in an explicitly sexual statement of ownership, women were branded on the breast. Owners used the same, or similar, branding irons to stamp their mark of ownership on their cattle and horses as well as to ensure their return should they stray. In effect, the branding of newly enslaved people was intended to serve precisely the same purposes. The brand mark was a visible statement, both to them and to the world at large, that they were considered of no more and no less worth than any other beasts of burden.

It was not just with the branding iron that many planters sought to deny both the humanity and the individual personalities of the slaves. What was often done arbitrarily, but sometimes intended to mock and humiliate the slaves, their owners stripped them of their original African names and renamed them in much the same way as they named their dogs and horses. The intent of owners was clear enough. They wished to exercise complete domination, to secure the same unthinking, blind obedience from these women and men as they did from their domesticated animals. From their perspective, their ideal relationship with the enslaved people they acquired, regardless of their number, age, or gender, would be one that was utterly non-negotiable. Almost immediately, they would be forced to admit that such an ideal was simply unattainable. This was evident in the way in which some slaves reacted to attempts to rename them. They clung to their original African names, and often named their children according to African practices. The African tradition of naming a child after the day of the week upon which it had been born persisted for many decades in the American South. For example, as in Africa, boys born on Sundays were often called Quashie, or Quash; girls born on Thursdays might be named Abba. Despite their wishes, then, the naming of slave babies was one highly significant way in which owners found themselves being forced to concede to those whose bodies and minds they sought to totally dominate.

Very soon after their arrival in their new American homes, whether in New England or the southern mainland, in towns or in the countryside, enslaved women and men discovered the real reason why they had been forcibly removed from Africa. That Europeans wanted their bodies was true enough, but they wanted work from those bodies rather than to eat them as the slaves had feared. The different working environments into which newly enslaved people had been plunged would be a fundamental determinant both of the new lives that their owners intended for them and the new lives that they struggled to carve out for themselves.

# CHAPTER THREE

∼

# Worlds of Work

What the American colonists required from the thousands upon thousands of Africans who were made available to them via the transatlantic slave trade was work. By the late seventeenth century, slave work had come to be seen as indispensable by white southerners, and they were not wrong in assuming that their ever-increasing prosperity depended upon the often brutal exploitation of people of African descent.

By the mid-eighteenth century, in their legal capacity as property, slaves had come to represent a significant proportion of the wealth claimed by the colonists, especially by those living in the southern region. In their capacity as workers, they contributed in innumerable ways to the economic well-being of those who owned and employed them and many others who hired their services. The northern colonies were never as dependent on enslaved workers as were those to the south of Pennsylvania, but even so, beginning in the late 1630s slaves occupied important niches in their evolving economies.

Slave work varied considerably both within and between the different regions of the mainland, but there were significant similarities as well as equally significant differences in the kinds of work slaves performed. From the time of the arrival of the first Africans in Virginia, the overwhelming majority of slaves, everywhere in the mainland, were put to work as agricultural laborers. Although agricultural systems sometimes involved similar tasks, for example, hoeing or weeding, they differed significantly according to the natural environment in which the slaves found themselves.

In New England, for example, where export staples such as tobacco and rice could not be grown, slaves worked as laborers on the small, mixed-family farms that came to characterize that region. In practice, this usually meant three things. First, these farms generated neither the need nor the capital to

31

employ more labor than that which could be supplied by the owner's family and, depending upon the size of the operation, perhaps one or two additional permanent hands. Second, many, and probably most, black farmhands found themselves virtually isolated from other enslaved people during the work week. They were also likely to find themselves not only taking orders from their owners but also working alongside them for much, if not all, of that time. On the one hand, this close proximity of owner and slave generated a degree of familiarity that might have resulted in more benign treatment. Yet these continual close contacts meant that in New England enslaved farmhands enjoyed comparatively little privacy.

Finally, there was the kind of agricultural work required of enslaved workers on these mixed farms. Most of the slaves performed all of the tasks associated with the production of various grains and root crops, and on many farms they would also be required to tend to livestock and poultry. Whenever time permitted, and whenever it was required, they would clear land as well as perform repair work on fences and various farm buildings. After all, it made no financial sense to call in a specialist, assuming that one was readily available, when the farmer and his black hand or hands could do the work themselves. Like many of their owners, black farmhands in New England found themselves becoming the jack of if not all, then certainly of many, skilled and semiskilled trades, such as carpentry and blacksmithing.

What was true of New England was also broadly true of the other regions of the mainland, including the tobacco-producing area of the Chesapeake and the rice swamps of South Carolina and Georgia. In these areas small family farms, perhaps employing one or two enslaved workers, coexisted alongside larger estates that might make use of as many as a hundred slaves. However, such large slaveholdings were the exception rather than the rule. On most tobacco- and rice-producing plantations, the enslaved workforce numbered somewhere between ten and fifty people. Yet whatever their size, there were some important similarities as well as some important differences in the working lives of slaves on tobacco and rice plantations.

As long as tobacco and rice planters remained largely dependent upon the transatlantic slave trade for the bulk of their workers, most slaves entered their new worlds of work as adults. But with the emergence of slave families, and the beginnings of natural reproduction, a growing number entered the world of work as children. When they reached the age of six or seven, enslaved boys and girls would be put to work at various light tasks around the plantation. For example, they might be sent to the rice or tobacco fields where they would be made to act as human scarecrows. From the outset, there was absolutely no doubt as to what kinds of work would be demanded of them as they grew older. Once they reached the age of about ten or eleven, slave boys and girls were usually considered ready and able to become part of the adult world of work. What this meant, both in the Chesapeake and in the lowcountry, was that unless and until they became physically incapable of working, they would spend the rest of their lives as field hands.

Everywhere in the southern mainland, and regardless of the size of the plantation upon which they lived, the majority of slaves were employed as field hands. This meant doing often backbreaking, and sometimes physically dangerous, work for six days a week throughout the year. However, most owners gave their slaves a few days off work after harvest and at Christmastime.

By the 1730s and 1740s, one of the most important differences between the plantation regimes of the Chesapeake tidewater and the Carolina lowcountry was in the ways in which planters organized their slave workforces. In the Chesapeake, tobacco planters favored what came to be known as the gang system. As its name suggests, this meant that slaves worked together in groups, or gangs, of various sizes. These gangs were made to labor from dawn to dusk, but were allowed short breaks for meals.

The task system, a very different system of organizing fieldwork, evolved in the lowcountry. There, depending upon their age and gender, slaves were assigned a particular task, or tasks, that had to be completed during the course of the day. Once the task had been completed to the satisfaction of the owner or overseer, the convention was that no more work would be required of the slaves until the following day. Unlike the gang system, the task system had a crucially important incentive built into it: the prospect of free time. The faster the task was completed, the more free time the slave had at his or her disposal.

Although there was a fundamental difference in the ways in which the work of field hands was organized by tobacco and rice planters, there were also some similarities in the kinds of work that the slaves were made to do and the ways in which that work was supervised. Everywhere in the southern mainland, female slaves used as field hands did much the same kinds of work as did enslaved men. They hoed the fields, they planted and harvested the crop, and often assisted men in what could be the extremely heavy work involved in land clearance. Neither menstruation nor pregnancy and childbirth necessarily granted them exemption from work. Another similarity between the Chesapeake tidewater and the Carolina lowcountry was the way in which the work of field hands was supervised. On smaller estates, fieldwork tended to be supervised by owners who, as was the case on many northern farms, often worked alongside their slaves.

On larger estates, or where owners had more than one plantation, overseers were hired to take on that role. Eminent planters might visit the fields periodically to check up on things, but most were content to let their overseers assume the daily responsibility for organizing and supervising the work of their field hands. Almost without exception, this was true of the significant number of prominent women planters in the colonial South, who had inherited land and slaves as the result of their husband's death.

Sometimes planters secured the services of an overseer through word of mouth. On other occasions, they advertised their need in a local newspaper. Whichever method they followed, owners often stated that they preferred a married man. There were two main reasons why they did so. First, there was the possibility that a single man might seek to form a sexual relationship, or relationships, with female slaves whose work he supervised. Owners were not particularly concerned with the sexual mores of these women, or with helping them to secure and safeguard the right to sexual protection. What did bother them, though, were the possible discontent, jealousies, and potential disorder that such sexual relationships might cause in the slave quarters. When such disorders did occur, owners were by no means reluctant to fire the overseer concerned. Rightly or wrongly, many owners believed that the presence of a wife might keep her overseer husband on the sexual straight and narrow. Second, they appreciated that by hiring a married man they were getting two employees for the price of one. Overseers' wives could take charge of the poultry and supervise work in the dairies that were found on most plantations.

Most overseers were hired by the year, and their record during that time determined whether or not they would be kept on. What this meant in practice, of course, was the size and quality of the crop that had been produced under their supervision, which in turn meant how effective they had been in managing the slave workforce. And here, they could find themselves in something of a bind.

Overseers' jobs depended upon them being able to find the best means of persuading enslaved field hands to work efficiently and productively. The use of the whip, sometimes lavishly, was one way of doing that, but it was not necessarily to the overseer's advantage to use this method indiscriminately. After all, slaves were valuable capital assets, and it was scarcely in their owners' interest that they be scarred and possibly maimed for life by punishments inflicted by overseers. Such injuries could scarcely be kept hidden from owners and, in some cases, were actually reported directly to them by trusted slaves. Thus, if an overseer wished to keep his job for more than a year, he had to tread very carefully.

On some larger plantations, owners and overseers were assisted by men who in many ways had an even more difficult job than they did, enslaved drivers. In effect, the driver was something of a middle man between the field hands and the owner or overseer. It was his job to ensure that field hands worked at a satisfactory pace, and he was authorized to use force to ensure that this pace was achieved. The records tell us virtually nothing about either the readiness of drivers to use the whip or the extent to which they were willing and able to exploit their position to obtain concessions for the field hands who worked under their supervision.

The planter ideal was that both the maximization of their profits and the prevention of organized slave resistance depended upon the constant supervision of the slaves' work by either themselves or by paid overseers. However, there were times when groups of slaves, as well as individual slaves, were left to work unsupervised. This might be a temporary arrangement caused by the illness, death, or temporary absence of the owner or overseer. In other instances it was because it was simply impracticable to closely supervise the work being done by the slaves. For example, some slave men were employed as shepherds and cow herders, work that often took them some distance from the main plantation. Sometimes with and sometimes without their owners, other male slaves were employed in the frontier regions as traders and trappers. Yet whatever their occupations, slaves who worked unsupervised always faced the prospect of harsh physical punishment if they failed to live up to the trust placed in them by their owners.

Regardless of whether they employed overseers and drivers, tobacco and rice planters were determined to maximize their profits. This meant minimizing their production costs and getting as much work as they could out of their enslaved hands. But what incentive did those hands have to work as hard as their owners demanded, or even to work at all? However hard they worked and however much money they made for their owners, they would reap few personal rewards. Their work might secure them a few material benefits in the form of food and clothing, but it did not secure them their freedom from bondage. In every part of the southern mainland, the main incentive to work, and to work hard enough to satisfy the demands made by owners, came in the shape of physical coercion.

The whip was the most visible symbol of the authority claimed by southern planters, and there is plenty of evidence to show that they did not hesitate to use it. For example, there are many descriptions of slaves that include details of the scars that stayed with them long after they had been whipped. Of course, not every field hand had to be viciously whipped in order for the owner or overseer's point to be made. The mere threat of a whipping, especially if one had been forced to watch the flogging of another worker, who might have been a close friend or even a family member, could be enough for owners or overseers to get their way, at least for the time being.

Moreover, it was not in the owners' interest to whip their field hands to the point where they were physically incapable of work, let alone to the point where their capital value was severely diminished by the scars they bore. Inevitably, those scars suggested to prospective buyers that they were reluctant workers and troublemakers. Of course, these scars probably suggested something entirely different to enslaved people: Here were men and women who had asserted themselves, who had stood up for themselves, and possibly for someone else, and who as a result had paid a horribly painful physical price for their assertiveness.

Enslaved field hands faced the constant threat of the whip, but this by no means meant that they were, or felt themselves to be, completely helpless in the face of the naked power that could be used against them by those who supervised their work. There were various ways in which they were able to assert themselves in their worlds of work and, in the process, wrench important concessions from their owners and overseers. For example, they might run away and return only when their demands had been met.

Although most slaves who lived on large tobacco or rice plantations worked in the fields, some did not. Like farmers further north in the mainland, southern planters had every financial incentive to be economically self-sufficient. In practice, this often meant that they trained some of the enslaved men and boys on their estates to work in various skilled and semi-skilled occupations. On many large plantations, for example, male slaves worked full time as blacksmiths, carpenters, coopers, and sawyers. Depending upon the locality, they were also employed in large numbers as boatmen and sailors and were mainly responsible for ferrying the plantation crops to the port towns from which they were exported to European markets.

These kinds of work offered some male slaves significant opportunities. For example, depending upon the local demand for their services, enslaved artisans and craftsmen might find themselves being hired out to ply their trade. This meant that at the same time as they were securing valuable income for their owners, they were also securing important information about life outside the immediate parameters of their home plantation. This information combined with their skills served them well if they ever thought about running away from their owners. But even if they decided not to run away, through their work these men enjoyed an important degree of quasi-autonomy that was denied to most field hands, male or female.

By the early eighteenth century a combination of wealth and social pretension was prompting many prominent tobacco and rice planters to seek another kind of work from a comparatively small number of their enslaved people: economically unproductive work in their households. Not least because they were stung by British criticisms of themselves as being uncouth and uncivilized provincials, wealthy planters were determined to demonstrate their taste and civility. They increasingly tried to do this in their material culture, in the clothing they wore, in the ways in which they furnished their houses, and in their fondness for having their portraits painted. They longed for nothing more than to be recognized, and fully appreciated, as having the taste, the manners, and the civility of English ladies and gentlemen.

It was as part and parcel of this process that planters began to imitate the Old World practice of employing some of their enslaved people as domestic servants. Not surprisingly, both in the Chesapeake tidewater and in the Carolina lowcountry, domestic service was gendered in a very traditional European fashion. Female slaves worked as cooks, cleaners, and personal maids to their mistresses, while enslaved men worked mainly for their masters as valets and grooms.

House slaves might seem to have been particularly privileged, compared with field hands, and in one sense this was probably true. They almost certainly received better food and clothing from their owners than did field hands, but at the cost of being at the constant beck and call of their masters and mistresses. There is no firm evidence to suggest either that they considered themselves to be a cut above field hands or that they were unconditionally loyal to the interests of their owners and their families. Like field hands, they took every opportunity that presented itself, and created whatever opportunities they could, to assert themselves and their individuality and to protect their own interests as well as those of their family and friends. Often those families and friends included field hands. Moreover, the number of reports of owners and their families being poisoned by their house slaves, by those whom they had previously considered entirely trustworthy, runs completely counter to the notion that these women and men were uncritically devoted to those who held them in captivity.

Whereas in the southern countryside only a tiny number of enslaved women and men worked within their owners' households, the opposite tended to be the case in towns, northern as well as southern. In towns as far apart as Boston and Charleston, slave occupations were virtually identical. Male slaves performed a wide range of skilled and semiskilled, as well as unskilled, jobs in the mainland colonies' rapidly developing urban economies. For example, in every port town male slaves worked around the docks, helping to load and unload boats and transporting goods around the town. In these towns, as well as those which were landlocked, enslaved men were also to be found plying virtually every trade and craft. They worked as carpenters, brick makers, and joiners. Some were employed as blacksmiths, farriers, and ships' chandlers. Yet others painted and decorated houses, or swept their chimneys, and there were also those who made jewelry and furniture of the very highest and most sought-after quality. For many, if not most, of these men, it meant that they had served an apprenticeship. Very often they had been taught their trade by their owners, and after the completion of their apprenticeship they continued to work alongside them.

In the countryside and in the towns, with one or two gendered exceptions, trades and crafts were effectively closed to slave women. Those that were open to some of them were the traditional female employments of sewing and millinery. In every colonial town, there were two main forms of employment open to female slaves. The first, and that which occupied most of them, was domestic work identical to that performed by enslaved women in southern plantation houses. The second was marketing.

By the mid-eighteenth century, female slaves were already beginning to dominate the public markets of southern towns such as Charleston, and they were also to be found, in smaller numbers, in those of the larger urban centers of New England and the Middle Atlantic colonies. Owners often employed slaves to take such things as fruit and vegetables, fish, meat, and dairy produce to market and trusted them to return with whatever money they had managed to make. The evidence suggests that, as was also the case in both European and west African towns, marketing was gendered, with women being mainly responsible for selling garden produce and dairy products and men for selling meat. Public markets were also gendered in another way. Most of those who went to them to buy food were women, and in the southern towns this meant mainly enslaved women.

Urban markets were one of the most important public spaces open to slaves, and to a significant extent they became public spaces that were dominated by women. They also provided spaces in which enslaved people from the countryside encountered those who lived in towns. These were spaces in which news and information were, where new friendships formed and old ones were reinforced, and where rebellious action could be talked about and planned.

Everywhere in the mainland, the context in which slaves performed their daily work was one of the most important differences between urban and rural slavery, and these contexts were clearly gendered. Female slaves, who worked as domestics in the towns, and this meant the majority of them, might be sent out on errands, but in most cases their jobs required that they spend much of their time within their owner's household. It was different for men. In the towns, skilled and semiskilled male slaves often worked alongside, and under the immediate supervision, of their owners; but most unskilled male workers, which meant most enslaved men, did not. For example, those who lived in a port town, and who worked around the docks as casual laborers, spent much, if not most, of the working day away from their owners. Very often they were sent off to hire themselves out and to return at the end of the day, or at the end of the week, with a predetermined amount of money for their owner. Any extra they made was theirs to keep and to spend or to save as they pleased.

That the employment of enslaved people made a significant contribution to the overall economic health of colonial towns in the north and south is readily evident. Moreover, the urban environments, and the greater freedom of movement and association they offered, provided enslaved people with many opportunities denied to the majority of those who lived and worked in the countryside. As events in New York City in 1712, and again in 1741, so clearly revealed, those opportunities included the possibility of organizing and implementing bloody uprisings. These two rebellions were crushed with comparative ease by the town's white authorities, but they brought home to white townspeople the nature of the risk they ran by placing such reliance upon enslaved workers. By and large, though, and for exactly the same mixture of economic and racial reasons that operated in the towns and countryside of the southern colonies, this was a risk that northern townspeople, just as much as white southerners, remained willing to take for the remainder of the colonial period.

Throughout the colonial period, all the mainland colonies were rural, agricultural societies with around 90 percent of the total population living on, and earning their living from, the land. Beginning in the mid-seventeenth century, enslaved black workers came to be seen as essential to the profitable production of such export crops as tobacco and rice, and by the early eighteenth century they performed virtually all of the jobs associated with the growth of these commodities. The forced labor of enslaved black people was the basis of the wealth enjoyed by southern planters. Slave labor was far less important in the agricultural regimes of the New England and Middle Atlantic states than it was in places like Virginia and South Carolina. However, the northern colonists did benefit both directly and indirectly from black slavery. Some northerners made a great deal of money from the transatlantic slave trade, as well as by shipping the tobacco and rice produced in the southern colonies to European markets. Moreover, enslaved workers filled many slots in the rapidly expanding urban economies of places such as Boston, New York, and Philadelphia.

Of course, in many ways the daily life of an enslaved field hand—male or female—working in the rice swamps of South Carolina and a carpenter or ladies' maid working in Philadelphia could not have been more different. But there were similarities, for example, between the kinds of work done by a carpenter or a ladies' maid in Philadelphia and their counterparts in Charleston, South Carolina. Depending upon where they lived, and their gender, difference and similarity marked the working lives of enslaved people. Exactly the same would be true of other aspects of their lives, not least the family and religious lives they struggled to build for themselves.

# CHAPTER FOUR

# Family Lives

Seldom, if ever, did the different ways in which African peoples were obtained for the transatlantic slave trade pay any regard to their family structures and relationships, to the feelings between husband and wife, or to the love between parents and their children. Often it was a matter of pure chance if members of the same family found themselves being loaded onto the same slave ship. Usually, boarding a slave ship meant being permanently separated from one's immediate family. The sense of personal loss, and the sorrow and desperation that such separations must have entailed both to those who were taken and to those who remained in Africa, can barely be imagined.

Yet the traumatic experience of the Middle Passage destroyed neither the memory of family nor the very basic human need for emotional and sexual companionship. From the outset, everywhere in the mainland colonies, and often against the most appalling odds, enslaved African peoples sought to form and maintain such relationships. At different times and at different rates, marriage and the family emerged as the essential building blocks of evolving slave communities. Indeed, marriage, family, and the formation of kinship networks became the glue that held those communities together. The family also became one of the major battlefields between owners and enslaved people, as the latter fought to secure all the rights normally associated with a secure family life. Those rights included being able to choose a marriage partner and to remain with that partner as well as with any children born to that partnership.

In none of the mainland colonies did enslaved people have a legally established right to either marriage or parenthood. In practice, evolving patterns of marriage, family formation, and parenthood depended upon two things: the availability of marriage partners in any given locality, that is to say not only the number but also the age structure and sex ratio of the local slave population; and the influence that owners were able to exert over patterns of courtship and marriage and, in time, over the family as well as evolving kinship networks.

The relatively small number and dispersal of enslaved people in the New England and Middle Atlantic colonies meant that, outside major towns such as Boston, New York, and Philadelphia, the choice of a marriage partner was somewhat restricted. Further south, in the plantation colonies, choices might also be restricted, but here it would be for rather different reasons, having mainly to do with the attitudes of slave owners.

Beginning in the late seventeenth century in the southern colonies, most slaves lived on farms or plantations worked by fewer than twenty hands. Moreover, until the mid-eighteenth century in the Virginia tidewater, and for longer in the Carolina lowcountry, while the transatlantic slave trade still operated, there was a marked gender imbalance, with male slaves sometimes heavily outnumbering females. Not surprisingly, this could and did produce fierce competition between enslaved men for those women who were available as sex partners. Whether the women concerned felt empowered, or threatened, by this competition, how much choice they had in selecting a partner, and the extent to which they may have played one suitor off against another, is open to conjecture. About this, as about so many other aspects of their lives, we have no record of their thoughts, of their hopes, and of their fears.

We do know that for essentially practical reasons, southern slave owners often sought to actively intervene in enslaved peoples' patterns of courtship and marriage. What this could mean in practice was that male and female slaves who lived on larger estates were encouraged to form sexual partnerships with one another. The reason why such partnerships were advantageous to owners, and why they had a vested interest in trying to prevent enslaved people seeking marriage partners on neighboring estates, had to do with visiting. By tacitly acknowledging the bonds of affection between slave couples who had chosen to be together, owners believed that husbands and wives who lived on different estates would try to be together as often as they possibly could. The same would be true of enslaved fathers whose children lived with their mother on a nearby plantation. Such visits might be made after the day's work, during the hours of darkness, when there would be no loss of income to the owners. But, as time was to prove, enslaved people might try to convert these short visits into more permanent arrangements by persuading their spouse, perhaps with the help of other trustworthy slaves, to hide them on the plantation. If this happened, then there would be a loss, and potentially a costly loss, of the enslaved person's labor during the time that he or she was absent. Nevertheless, with or without the permission of their owners, the slaves determined to forge relationships with men and women of their own choosing, with men and women whom they loved, and they often sought and found marriage partners on neighboring plantations.

The records for the colonial period remain largely silent on the number and proportion of marriages that took place between slaves. Similarly, there is very little surviving evidence about patterns of courtship, the various rituals associated with marriage, or the extent to which African patterns of marriage survived, and if so for how long, in different parts of the North American mainland.

Reports sent to London by the Anglican, or Episcopalian, clergy of Virginia and South Carolina around the turn of the eighteenth century suggest that what were sometimes referred to as "double marriages" were commonplace. This mirrored the practice in some parts of Africa, where men were said by Europeans to be taking more than one wife. There are also snippets of evidence from the mid-eighteenth-century South that courtship and the marriage ceremony involved various forms of gift giving as well. Unfortunately, white commentators did not record the precise details of the marriage ritual, of what was said and done by the couple concerned, and who conducted the ceremony. The feasting and music making widely associated with slave weddings was not a distinct characteristic of Africa. European and colonial American marriages also involved music and the provision of food and drink for the couple's family and friends.

However, the erroneous impression of white reporters, and especially of Anglican clergymen, was that slave marriages were essentially casual affairs, that enslaved husbands and wives separated frequently, as and when they felt like it, and that nothing could be further removed from the Christian ideal of monogamous marriage than those that they were entering into. The few Anglican ministers who tried to persuade slaves to abandon their own marriage patterns in favor of the Christian model were generally unsuccessful.

Whatever forms their marriage ceremonies took, and regardless of whether or not they engaged in double marriages, slave couples had absolutely no guarantee that theirs would be a lifetime relationship. In theory, that relationship was under the complete control and domination of their owners, and it was a relationship that could be destroyed at any time and for any reason. In their legal capacity as property, enslaved people could be sold, given away in wills or as gifts, and even gambled away. At no point could a slave couple be absolutely certain that they would always be able to remain together. One of the greatest risks of being forcibly separated came in the immediate aftermath of their owner's death. This was the point at which they might find themselves bequeathed to different members of his or her family. In some cases, their new owners lived locally, which meant visiting spouses or other family members was a possibility, but this was not always the case. Saved couples also ran the risk of being sold apart for no other reason than the need or greed of their owner. Some slaves were disposed of in order to repay a debt or sold because an offer had been made for them that was too good to be refused.

We will never be able to know for certain exactly how many couples were forcibly separated by inheritance or through sale, but three sources in particular suggest that this was by no means an uncommon occurrence. The advertisements for enslaved runaways, which by the 1730s were beginning to be placed in newspapers published in towns as far apart as Boston and Charleston, indicate that a significant proportion of those who took flight did so in order to be reunited with a spouse. Similarly, slave owners' wills also testify to a readiness to part husbands and wives, as do the records that detail both the slaves' private sale as well as their public auction.

Although enslaved couples could never be entirely certain that they would be allowed to remain together, they were able to assert themselves in ways that could lessen that possibility. Everywhere in the mainland, the fact, or threat, of taking flight was arguably the most potent weapon available to enslaved husbands and wives who had been separated against their will. Sometimes, and with varying degrees of success, slave couples might plead with their owner, or seek the intervention of a local clergyman to prevent them being sold apart.

Enslaved couples struggled, and not always in vain, to secure the right to remain together and to remain for as long as they possibly could with any children who were born to them. Slave owners, of course, fully appreciated the reproductive value of enslaved women. Given that the legal status of the child followed that of its mother, every slave child represented a potentially lucrative capital asset as well as a potentially valuable worker. In view of this financial incentive it might be expected that owners made special provisions for pregnant women, for example, by lightening their work loads during their pregnancy and giving them sufficient time off work to recover after giving birth; but neither of these things happened. In the plantation colonies of the South, for example, pregnant field hands were often made to work at backbreaking jobs up until just before they gave birth and, unless there were serious complications, they returned to the fields within a day or two afterward. Sometimes, following a traditional African practice, they worked in the fields with their babies strapped to their backs. As children grew too big to be carried in this way, they could be looked after by female slaves who were too old to do heavy fieldwork. The convention among planters was that they would not forcibly separate mothers from their children by selling them apart until the latter reached the age of seven or eight years old.

It is impossible to say how many enslaved mothers, particularly field hands, either lost their unborn children through miscarriages brought about by the hard physical work demanded of them or aborted their babies in order to save them from a life of bondage. Most mothers suckled their children for up to two or three years, hoping thereby to avoid pregnancy during that time. Although the evidence is sketchy, two things are clear: the love that slave mothers and fathers felt for their children, and the ways in which they sought to instill in them at least some remembrance of their African past. The initial and one of the most significant reminders of continuity between Africa and America was the ways in which slave parents named their children.

Unless newly imported slaves had an African name that could be easily transliterated into English—Kweni might become Queen or Queenie and Cudjoe shortened to Joe—they were likely to be stripped of their given names, which often carried an enormous spiritual significance. Sometimes, if they refused to acknowledge the English names bestowed upon them by their colonial owners, newly enslaved people were beaten unmercifully until they were willing to do so. But when it came to naming their own children, slave parents looked to their African pasts and turned to African naming practices for guidance. The persistence of Islam in the mainland colonies is suggested by parents naming their sons after the prophet Mohamed. Many parents, whose religious beliefs are not recorded, named their child after the day of the week upon which it was born, as they had done in Africa. Over perhaps two or three generations, these names might become corrupted into English versions of the African original, a process that was part and parcel of the dynamics of the process of becoming African American instead of just African. Exactly the same was true of a second aspect of the naming process. Sometimes parents named their children after close family members of theirs who remained in Africa. As kinship networks began to develop in America, children might be named after an American-born relative, such as an aunt or uncle.

In many ways, of course, the determination of slave parents that it should be they, rather than their owners, who named any children born to them was indicative of the battle that would be waged over the enslaved child's future. At issue was the question of whose influence over the child's development would carry most authority. From the child's perspective, during the first five or six years of life the parental, but in the case of many separated parents primarily the maternal, influence would be most immediate and most significant. At the age of five or six, though, it was highly likely that the enslaved child would start to be made aware of what the future held for him or her. Even in play, the child might be beaten for raising a hand to, let alone hitting, a white child. Similarly, it was at this same young age that the child was introduced to the world of adult work and made to carry out light tasks around the estate. What enslaved parents sought to do was to prepare their children to physically and emotionally survive in that world.

For varying lengths of time, slave children lived with their mothers and their fathers, if they lived on the same estate, in a single household, the slave cabin, which was generally roughly constructed mainly of wood and sometimes clay. Usually built by the slaves themselves, the cabin consisted of one or possibly two rooms. This was the slave family's semiprivate space, where they enjoyed a certain amount of independence from their owners.

Evidence suggests that slave cabins were sparsely furnished, often with furniture and cooking utensils that either had been made by slaves, usually by enslaved husbands, or had been purchased with the pitiful amounts of money that the husband and wife had managed to make by working for themselves, or by selling commodities they had produced or acquired, during the time that they were not required to work for their owners.

Between the late seventeenth and the mid-eighteenth centuries, the various kinds of employment undertaken by enslaved people during their so-called leisure time formed the basis of what are often known as their household, domestic, or informal economies. In many parts of the plantation south, owners sought to trim their costs by providing enslaved people with minimal amounts of food and clothing. For example, they might issue their field hands with two sets of clothing per year, one for the summer and one for the winter months. For men, this usually meant being given trousers and a shirt, while most women were given a skirt or wrap. Many slaves were forced to go barefoot. Typically, the food issued by owners, often on a weekly basis, included corn and sometimes a piece of pork. If slaves wanted to improve this basic standard of living, then they had little alternative but to work during their own time to do so.

Southern planters often set aside patches of land for enslaved people to supplement their nutrition. These gardens became the basis of the slaves' domestic economies. Initially owners hoped that the slaves would use their gardens to grow just enough fruit and vegetables to satisfy their own immediate needs. Very soon, though, the slaves produced surpluses, and this raised the thorny issue of who they belonged to and how they would be disposed of.

By the early eighteenth century, plantation slaves were well on the way toward securing an extremely important right from their owners: the right to claim as their own property any commodities that they managed to produce during their own time. These commodities included not only garden produce, which almost certainly involved a cooperative effort on the part of the enslaved family, but also a range of other goods that clearly reflected a division of labor within the enslaved household. For example, most of the fish and game that featured in the slaves' diets, and that they sometimes offered for sale, had been caught or trapped by men. Likewise the slaves' furniture, boxes, and canoes that slaves had to dispose of were also made by men.

Owners appreciated that if they tried to claim any of these commodities as their own they would be stirring up discontent in the slave quarters, and the last thing they wanted was resentful slaves. However, while they conceded the right of ownership, they tried to control the disposal of these goods. Some slave owners did this by offering to value and sell the commodities produced by the slaves in exchange for providing them with the things they sought. Although the records are fragmentary, they give us a good idea of what those things were. Slaves tried to supplement their diets by requesting such things as sugar and molasses. They sought metal-ware pots and pans for their cabins and bought either cloth or ready-made clothes to wear on special occasions as an alternative to the basic uniforms provided by their owners. It seems reasonable to suggest that these purchases reflected joint decision making on the part of enslaved husbands and wives.

Slaves did not confine their buying, selling, and bartering activities to deals that they negotiated with their owners. Showing a remarkable degree of resourcefulness, they managed to forge links with local white people, who were often willing to break the laws forbidding them to trade with slaves. Depending upon where they lived, slaves might also be able to sell or barter their goods in the public market of a nearby town and buy what they wanted from amenable shopkeepers.

Born originally perhaps from a desperate need to do whatever it took to ensure the immediate physical well-being, if not the very survival, of themselves and their families, slaves displayed a considerable amount of ingenuity, and expended an equal amount of energy, in the forging and maintenance of their household economies. But these were economies whose significance cannot be measured simply and solely in monetary or material terms. They were also economies that from the outset demonstrated the strength of the ties of affection that both united and strengthened the enslaved family.

Of course, to emphasize the strength of the slave family is to run the risk of thereby romanticizing it and underestimating the significance of the stresses and strains that always confronted it. Indisputably, the gravest external threat to the family and relationships within it came from the owners' authority. Much depended upon enslaved peoples' success in being able to blunt that authority. Sometimes they were able to do so, for example, by persuading their owners not to sell them apart, but on many other occasions they were not.

It would also be foolish and wrong to convey the impression that relations within the slave family were always placid and supportive, because they were not. There were times, as there have always been times within every family, when husbands and wives, parents and children, fell out with one another, when harsh words were spoken and perhaps even blows were exchanged. Sometimes husbands and wives were sexually unfaithful to one another, and sometimes they separated not because they were forced to by their owners but because they themselves wished to live apart. It would have been truly remarkable had this not been so. However, their families were always the source of enormous strength to enslaved people.

CHAPTER FIVE

# Religious Lives

Given the nature of the transatlantic slave trade, it was unlikely that west and west central African religious beliefs and practices could have fully survived the Middle Passage and that slaves could have re-created them exactly in British America. Yet capture and sale in Africa, followed by the sheer physical and emotional horrors of the Middle Passage, did not erase individual and group memories of those religious beliefs and practices. It did not necessarily undermine the often deeply held religious beliefs of those who found themselves in the holds of the slave ships. Moreover, it did not wipe out all those sacred specialists who might have been on board them who were held in such enormous esteem in African religious cultures. In view of their situation, some people may well have abandoned their religious faith, but for many others it was their faith, and the sheer unbreakable strength of that faith, that sustained them not only on the transatlantic crossing but also for long after their arrival in British America.

The main problem in attempting to unravel the dynamics of the reworking of traditional beliefs and rituals in different regions of mainland America, and the forms that they eventually took, is the lack of sources. Autobiographies and other materials written by former slaves only began to appear during the second half of the eighteenth century, which means that for the entire colonial period there are only white accounts of varying degrees of objectivity. Moreover, those accounts are relatively few and far between. Slave owners, the clergy, and other whites seem to have been disinterested in African religious practices and practitioners, except on those occasions when they found them sufficiently threatening, appalling, or amusing enough to write about.

However, these fragmentary records indicate that everywhere in seventeenth- and early-eighteenth-century British America, enslaved African peoples struggled, often against the most appalling odds, to translate their deeply held religious beliefs into concrete institutional forms. They tried to reconstruct as best they could the familiar religious rites and rituals they had known in their African homes. What European writers often failed to report was that those rites and rituals included those associated with Islam. Due to a combination of trade and military conquest, Islam had spread from the more northerly parts of Africa into the western and west central parts of the continent, into precisely those regions from which people were being fed into the transatlantic slave trade. Although the numbers will never be known for certain, Muslims found themselves being shipped into different parts of British America, but mainly to the plantation colonies.

The extent to which Muslims, as well as those professing different beliefs, were able to use their ancestral religious beliefs as blueprints for developing ritualistic practices for marrying, naming their children, and burying the dead, as well as for devising mutually acceptable codes of individual and group morality, depended upon a cluster of variables that differed over time and from place to place. Much depended upon the African backgrounds of the enslaved people in any given locality; their number, age, and gender; and the ease and frequency with which they could meet one another away from the prying eyes of their owners and other whites. The extent to which they were confronted by white attempts to persuade them to abandon their traditional religious cultures, including their religious leaders, in favor of the Christianity of their European owners was also crucially important.

One of the earliest clues about the determination of enslaved people in the southern colonies to reconstruct familiar religious practices concerns burials, and comes from late-seventeenth-century Virginia. In the late 1680s, Virginia's authorities expressed alarm about the fact that significant numbers of slaves were meeting at night in order to bury their dead. Nighttime burials occurred in parts of Africa, but in Virginia and other parts of the South, this might also have been because planters were unwilling to allow their slaves time off during the working day to bury their dead. Owners did not mention what form slave burials took. What concerned them was not so much the burial rituals devised by slaves as the possibility that such gatherings might provide the mourners with ideal opportunities to plot rebellion.

Evidence from the British Caribbean suggests that these burials entailed a funeral procession, with singing and instrumental music, and that various objects were buried with the body. These "grave goods" reflected a widespread African belief that after death the soul, or the spirit, returned home to Africa. Food and drink were buried with the body, or placed on top of the grave, to sustain the dead on the journey home. Sometimes grave goods included gifts for the family, friends, and ancestors who were believed to await them there. These burial practices did not necessarily reflect those of a single African religious culture. Depending upon the mix of the enslaved people in a particular locality, they involved a blending of mutually agreeable graveside ceremonies.

Equally brief descriptions from elsewhere in the mainland confirm both the persistence and the universality of the nighttime burials that so worried late-seventeenth-century Virginia planters. They also indicate that such burials were neither an exclusively rural phenomenon nor were they confined to the plantation colonies. They are known to have taken place in Boston and, on the eve of the American Revolution, Savannah authorities were complaining about enslaved people gathering during the hours of darkness to bury their dead. Neither rural slave patrols nor urban watches deterred mourners from going about their religious business.

Later evidence from the southern mainland, as well as from the colonial British Caribbean, strongly suggests that beginning in the seventeenth century enslaved people might well have engaged in another traditional African ritual involving the dead: the second funeral. This involved the family and friends of the deceased gathering at the graveside some weeks or months after the burial, where they engaged in various ceremonial activities that included eating, drinking, and music making. In parts of the British Caribbean, and possibly also on the North American mainland, the remembrance and honoring of the dead became an annual event.

Slaves not only turned to their ancestral religious cultures when it came to burying their dead, they did exactly the same when it came to marrying the living. Beginning in the late seventeenth century, the Anglican clergy who operated in the southern colonies expressed their horror at the persistence of African marriage patterns that were totally at odds with the Christian ideal. Although they commented on such practices as double marriages, in which a man took two wives, they said virtually nothing about either the practice of courtship or the precise forms of the marriage ritual. There is some suggestion that in parts of the mid-eighteenth-century South, slave marriages were in some ways similar to Christian marriages, in that they involved the giving of gifts and were occasions for feasting, music making, and dancing.

We know virtually nothing about those who assumed the main responsibility for conducting the rituals associated with marriage and death or those who claimed, and exercised, religious authority in the evolving slave communities of the mainland colonies. In the British Caribbean sacred specialists, often known as Obeah-men or women, enjoyed an enormous amount of power and they had special gifts—not least their knowledge of uses to which a wide range of herbs and other plants could be put and their ability to cast spells. It was sometimes said enslaved people would rather defy their owners and overseers than offend the Obeah. However, they were men and women who at a time of need could provide the necessary means of protecting slave houses and gardens and love as well as herbal potions that could take the life of an enemy, be that enemy another slave or the plantation owner or overseer.

References to sacred specialists in the slave communities of the mainland colonies are few and far between. Sometimes southern planters described one of their slaves, usually a man, as being, or claiming to be, a doctor. The expertise of some slaves in the use of herbs and other plants was acknowledged in two very contrasting ways. Occasionally, the willingness of a slave to reveal to whites an herbal remedy that was unknown to them would be rewarded, sometimes with freedom. More often, though, during the first half of the eighteenth century it was the harmful uses to which slaves allegedly put their herbal skills that attracted most white attention. Owners and their families could never entirely rule out the possibility that they might be poisoned by their slaves.

Throughout the colonial period the secular authorities of the different colonies enacted legislation that had significant implications for the evolving religious lives of slaves. Such legislation, whether it be in the form of passed laws, which insisted that slaves must have written permission to leave their plantations, or attempts to curb the playing of drums, instruments that were particularly important in the rituals associated with death and marriage, was not designed specifically to root out religious ceremonies or to strip sacred specialists of their influence in order to replace them with Christian equivalents. The main intention was to prevent large numbers of slaves from different plantations gathering together during the hours of darkness. Beginning in the late seventeenth century, however, there were those in the mainland colonies who wished to root out what they described as the heathen religious beliefs and practices of slaves.

Despite the vocabulary of some colonial churchmen, the seventeenth century saw no organized effort on the part of any Protestant sect or denomination in British North America to systematically convert slaves and as part and parcel of that process, to strip them of their traditional African religious cultures. Nowhere in the mainland had the attempted conversion of slaves become enshrined as a matter of pressing public policy.

Not even in the deeply religious New England colonies was an, albeit fluctuating, interest in trying to convert Native Americans matched by a similar concern to do the same with that region's comparatively small black population. Beginning in the seventeenth century, Puritan leaders never completely denied either the humanity or the intellectual capacity of the Africans they enslaved to understand the basic tenets of their version of Christianity. What did concern many of them, however, and was arguably the main reason why they made no systematic attempt to convert their slaves, was their deep suspicion of, and aversion to, the blackness of these "strangers" in their midst.

By the end of the seventeenth century, at exactly the same time as New England's enslaved population was growing quite significantly, several Puritan leaders were becoming increasingly concerned with preserving what might be described as the racial purity of their congregations. They did not wish to deny what they believed to be the many benefits of Christianity to their slaves but, at the same time, they did not relish the thought of sizeable numbers of black converts flooding into their churches. The availability and content of the religious instruction offered to, or forced upon, slaves continued to depend upon the inclinations and consciences of individual masters and mistresses. As far as black converts were concerned, they could not automatically rely upon being welcomed into their owners' churches with open arms or being treated by their white coreligionists as absolute equals.

What was true of seventeenth-century New England was also true of every other mainland colony. In every Protestant sect and denomination it would be slave owners who assumed the lion's share of the responsibility for instructing enslaved people in the basics of Christianity. From Massachusetts in the north to Georgia in the south, there were some owners who took their obligations as Christian masters and mistresses very seriously. However, the records suggest that particularly in the southern colonies, such owners were few and far between, and that only a minuscule proportion of the slave population received formal instruction in the Anglican beliefs of their owners. At the very least, the small number of slaves who were instructed would have been taught the Lord's Prayer and the Ten Commandments.

Depending upon the inclination of their owners, religious instruction also involved teaching some slaves to read. By the turn of the seventeenth century, however, many white colonists, particularly in the South, were beginning to point out just how dangerous this was. As these critics pointed out, although it might be desirable for Protestants to be able to read, and thereby understand the Bible, to allow enslaved people to do so would simply be asking for trouble. While it was true that they would come across St. Paul's remarks about the obedience and loyalty demanded of Christian servants, they would also be able to read about Moses leading his people out of slavery. Moreover, there was no cast-iron guarantee that slaves would limit their reading to the Bible and other religious materials. They would also be able to read secular publications like some Bible passages that might prompt them to question or even actively challenge their slave status.

Protestant clergy as well as slave owners differed in their attitudes toward slave literacy, but during the first half of the eighteenth century, those who opposed it began to get their way. Prohibitions on teaching slaves to read and write began to appear in the public laws of most southern colonies. But in a sense, this was a classic case of closing the stable door some time after the horse had bolted. Once slaves had acquired reading and writing skills, be it from their owners or from a sympathetic clergyman, it would be impossible for them to be stripped of such skills. Moreover, these were skills that could be passed on within and between generations in the comparative privacy of the slave quarters.

Given the fierce punishments of slaves found guilty of using the ability to read or write for purposes of their own, these were skills that often remained hidden from white eyes. We will never know exactly how many enslaved people in the mainland colonies were able to read and write. What we do know, though, is that the opponents of slave literacy were proved absolutely right. Increasingly, slaves were able to employ talents that derived originally from well-intentioned attempts to convert them to Christianity for various subversive purposes: they wrote passes, or manumission papers, stating that they were legally free. They could also read newspapers and other publications that, by the 1760s, were beginning to include scathing critiques of the institution of slavery.

All the evidence indicates a strong regional bias in the spread of Christianity among the slaves of the British mainland colonies before the mid-eighteenth century. Not surprisingly, it was one that reflected the number and proportion of slaves among any given colonial population. More than anything else perhaps, it was the thought of what enslaved converts might do with the potentially powerful weapon of Christianity that shaped owners' attitudes. Predictably, it was in the southern colonies where owners were most fearful of the emergence of a widespread religious ideology that, sooner or later, might provide the basis for collective resistance that might topple them. For essentially practical reasons, they felt that they simply could not afford to permit the forging of new identities, and new loyalties, that were based in a shared Christianity.

The Congregationalist, Quaker, and Presbyterian slave owners of the New England and Middle Atlantic colonies, where slaves comprised a comparatively small proportion of the population, were rather more active when it came to the religious instruction of their slaves than were the Anglican planters of the South. As one Anglican clergyman who worked in Virginia during the 1670s bitterly complained to his superiors in England: "the vast majority of southern Anglican masters and mistresses were not merely indifferent but positively hostile to any to any and all attempts to convert their slaves." Twenty years later, similar reports were being written by Anglican missionaries in lowcountry South Carolina.

These reports from Virginia and South Carolina said that owners offered different reasons—in their view equally unconvincing excuses—for refusing to allow their slaves to be instructed in Christianity. Despite the continuing reassurances of the Anglican hierarchy in London, some planters continued to fall back on the traditional argument that as one Christian could not hold another Christian in perpetual bondage, conversion to Christianity necessarily demanded the manumission of enslaved converts. Others claimed that a shared religion might provide enslaved converts with an unacceptable degree of moral leverage in their dealings with their coreligionist owners. In addition, there were those who claimed that they simply could not afford to let their enslaved workers take time off in order to receive religious instruction. Most owners simply shrugged off the missionaries' threat of the divine punishment that awaited them—either in this world or the next—if they continued to disregard their Christian responsibilities toward their slaves and remained utterly unconvinced by their promise that conversion to Christianity would transform slaves into willing, docile, and more productive workers.

Anglican missionaries were absolutely right about the unconditional opposition of most southern Anglican planters to the conversion of their slaves, which continued largely unabated into the era of the American Revolution. In 1701 an English-inspired, and mainly English-funded, organized missionary movement got underway with the founding in London of The Society for the Propagation of the Gospel in Foreign Parts. The Society's objective was to promote Anglicanism, particularly in the British American colonies. The Anglican clergy sponsored by the Society were active, particularly in the southern colonies, for the rest of the colonial period, but their efforts bore comparatively little fruit. True, the records reveal that there were some black Anglicans, but by the 1750s and 1760s, Anglican missionaries in the Chesapeake colonies, as well as in South Carolina and Georgia, were still complaining about the very small numbers of slaves who were being sent to them for instruction.

Not surprisingly, religious education was one of the main aims of the handful of schools that Anglicans set up specifically for black children. But these institutions, which were established in Charleston, South Carolina, in 1742, and in Virginia and North Carolina during the 1750s and 1760s by the English-based charitable organization The Associates of the Late Reverend Dr. Thomas Bray, were of very limited significance. They never had more than twenty or thirty black pupils at any one time, and most were virtually defunct, or had already closed, by the eve of the American Revolution. Southern planters were just as opposed to the instruction of slave children as they were to that of enslaved adults.

By any measure, Anglican missionary activity in the southern colonies during the first half of the eighteenth century was remarkably unsuccessful. Nevertheless, Anglican ministers remained confident that, if only given the chance, they would be able to convert ever-increasing numbers of slaves. But they were seriously mistaken; they were simply deluding themselves. In their opinion, their missionary efforts were being deliberately hindered by Anglican masters and mistresses. Through the middle years of the eighteenth century, Anglican clergymen continued to insist that slaves wanted nothing more than to be allowed access to the Anglicanism of their owners. If only they were permitted to do so, they would willingly cast off their ancestral religious beliefs and practices. Nothing could have been further from the truth, at least as far as Anglicanism was concerned.

The reasons why Anglicanism appealed to so few slaves in the southern colonies are not hard to find. This version of Christianity sanctioned the continuation of chattel slavery, offering no prospect whatsoever of freedom. Slaves who converted to Anglicanism, and attended church, were made to sit as far away as possible from their coreligionist owners. Racially based divisions outside the church were both reflected and reinforced within it.

Before the 1740s and 1750s, Anglicanism scarcely posed a serious challenge to the traditionally based religious beliefs and rituals that were continuing to evolve and becoming ever more deeply rooted in the slave quarters of the southern mainland. Yet during the middle years of the eighteenth century those beliefs and rituals, as well as enslaved sacred specialists, came under an ever-growing challenge from another form of Protestantism. The religious revivals that got underway in the 1720s and 1730s in New England

and the Middle Atlantic colonies, and during the 1750s and 1760s in the southern mainland, known as "The First Great Awakening," marked the beginnings of what proved to be the most monumental change in the religious lives of slaves, leading to the emergence of modern African American Protestantism. Until the time of the American Revolution, this change, though, would be contested within enslaved communities as well as by many slave owners.

With the notable exception of Quakerism, all the major Protestant sects and denominations of the mainland colonies experienced revivals between the 1720s and the 1760s. These revivals had a deceptively simple purpose; they sought to revitalize and reinvigorate traditional forms of Protestant teaching that many colonists, including Protestant ministers, claimed were failing to meet the spiritual needs of church-goers. The regional contexts and crises in which these revivals sprang up varied from the New England of the late 1730s, which was experiencing a deep economic, fiscal, and social crisis, to the sluggish tobacco prices that were besetting the tobacco economy of the Virginia tidewater. Although evangelical Protestantism was not a homogeneous movement, developing as it did in different places, at different times, and within different denominations, the strands that emerged shared many characteristics. Evangelical Protestants universally emphasized the doctrine of salvation by faith alone, the terrors of hell, and the importance of a strict personal and communal moral code.

Evangelical missionaries first appeared among the slaves of the southern mainland, in the South Carolina lowcountry, in the late 1730s. The work of two of them in particular, John Wesley and George Whitefield, was vital in laying the groundwork for what was to follow. Both men were shocked by the failure of masters and mistresses who claimed to be Christians to convert their slaves. Both were deeply impressed by the eagerness with which slaves embraced their evangelical message. But why was it that, unlike Anglicanism, their message was so very attractive to enslaved men and women? The answers to this question are not hard to find. Both the content of the evangelical message and the manner in which it was presented appealed to slaves.

Evangelical preachers presented a hopeful message that emphasized human worth and dignity in this world and the promise of salvation in the next. The way in which this message was presented—the oral nature of evangelicalism—was in striking contrast to the methods employed by Anglican ministers. Preaching and teaching by word of mouth, and often the use of an intensely powerful oratory, were the foundations of the evangelical movement. This was a method of teaching and learning that positively encouraged the participation of Africans, many of whose traditional cultures were based upon oral communication. Evangelical Protestantism empowered enslaved people in a way that Anglicanism did not. The evangelical preachers treated them as equals, and talked with rather than to the slaves. Evangelical preach-ers encouraged slaves to participate in spiritual leadership as lay speakers and teachers. According to evangelicals, the sole qualification for the exercise of spiritual authority rested not on formal education, status, or gender, but on having experienced the spiritual rebirth of conversion. Enslaved women par-ticularly welcomed this interpretation as it echoed the recognized role that many of them had filled as spiritual leaders in Africa.

Evangelical Protestantism also seemed to offer certain kinds of protection to enslaved converts. The possibility of Christian marriage might prevent the separation of families and a common religion might also safeguard against the brutal physical punishments inflicted by owners. The rapid growth of biracial evangelical Methodist and Baptist congregations generated by the First Great Awakening, everywhere in the mainland but particularly in the South, provided the enslaved members of those congregations with a new and potentially invaluable arena in which they could carry on their struggle to secure basic human rights. Evangelical Protestantism, then, offered both a vital, empowering religious ideology and a practical religious framework that enabled enslaved converts to create a strong and orderly community for themselves.

Although the number of enslaved converts grew steadily during the quar-ter of a century before the American Revolution, this process of religious transformation was not entirely uncontested. It was challenged by many enslaved people, who had a strong preference for their traditional beliefs and rituals, as well as by many of their owners. On the eve of the Revolution, the majority of enslaved people still remained either firmly attached to their traditional religious beliefs and spiritual leaders or professed no religious beliefs at all.

A few slave owners were converted to evangelical Protestantism, some-times by those women and men they continued to hold in bondage, but most were horrified and often greatly alarmed by a process that seemed to be undermining the racial and social authority they sought to exercise outside the churches. They failed to recognize that although enslaved converts felt enormously empowered by their new religion the fact that they were making different religious choices could work to their owners' advantage. Anything that divided enslaved people—be it their different African origins or now their different religious choices—was in their owners' interest.

What owners saw, though, were not divisions that might serve them well. Instead they saw a unity and a degree of cooperation between white and black, free and slave, Baptists and Methodists that seemed to be undermining the racial barriers they had enshrined in their slave codes. The very language used by the members of biracial churches as they referred to one another as "Sister" and "Brother" threatened to turn the world outside those churches on its head. Yet owners were as powerless to stop the progress of evangelical Protestantism among the slave populations of the mainland as they had been to stop the practice of ancestral African religious rituals. Once evangelical Protestantism had been made available to slaves, initially by white preachers, they could transform it in ways that suited their own distinct needs, and there was virtually nothing that their owners could do about it.

The start of the American Revolution deeply disrupted many different aspects of the social and cultural fabric of the North American mainland, and religion was no exception. The religious transformation of slaves from their ancestral religious cultures to evangelical Protestant Christianity was not entirely halted by the war, but it was certainly interrupted during this time. The transformation would pick up again, but with much greater force, in the postwar years. Following the Declaration of Independence and the adoption of the American Constitution, slaves, particularly those in the southern states, struggled to come to terms with the fact that they were denied the liberty claimed on behalf of all men. All they had to look forward to, and would be made to endure for the foreseeable future, was a continuation of their bondage. Evangelical Protestantism offered a religious language of comfort and hope that helped enable them to confront and, over the next seventy-five years, to endure that future.

# CHAPTER SIX

# Resistance and Rebellion

In theory, according to the public laws of slavery, which the mainland colonies began to enact during the early years of the eighteenth century, enslaved women and men were under the complete domination of their owners. Yet as those same laws revealed only too clearly, nowhere in the mainland colonies did owners expect that theoretical domination to go completely unchallenged. Indeed, it is evident that they thought that both individually and collectively people of African descent, those whom they had defined as pieces of property, would offer the most violent resistance to their captors. In every colony, rebellion or attempted rebellion, as well as the murder or the attempted murder, of any white person was made punishable by death. Harsh punishments could also be expected by any slave, male or female, who struck a white person, who ran away, or who pilfered or destroyed goods belonging to their owner or to any other white person.

In what was the only gendered difference in the slave codes, any enslaved man who was found guilty of raping or attempting to rape a white woman would also be sentenced to death. This reflected the concern of elite white lawmakers to control the sexual behavior of white women, by preventing them from forming relationships with black men. It was deeply rooted in a stereotype of black men as sexual predators. Not surprisingly, colonial lawmakers failed to make the sexual abuse of an enslaved woman by a white man a punishable offense. In part this stemmed from a deep-seated and self-serving image of African women as sexual temptresses who simply bewitched helpless white men. Of course, it was also true that, regardless of the legal status of their father, any children born to enslaved women would inherit their status. Female slaves could claim no legal right whatsoever to their bodies, or to the protection of their bodies from any form of sexual mistreatment.

From the outset, from the 1620s and 1630s, people of African ancestry behaved in most of the ways expected of them by their owners. But they also sought to assert themselves and their individuality in physically less threatening ways, testifying to both their resourcefulness and determination. Far from being completely helpless, they managed to marshal an impressive array of weapons with which to resist the awesome power at the disposal of their owners.

Given what they knew of uprisings on board the slave ships, and about the serious revolts that periodically took place in the sugar colonies, it is scarcely surprising that what the English colonists feared most of all from their slaves was organized rebellion. In fact, the chances of this ever happening during the entire colonial period were very slight. The small number of slaves everywhere in the mainland colonies until the last quarter of the seventeenth century scarcely posed a major threat to a well-armed white majority. This situation did not change for the remainder of the colonial period, even in the southern mainland, where slaves became an ever-increasing proportion of the total population.

As the transatlantic slave trade to the southern mainland got underway during the late seventeenth century, newly enslaved people were put to work on plantations that usually contained no more than about twenty or thirty hands. As Olaudah Equiano's experience so poignantly demonstrated, a similar skin color did not necessarily mean a common language. If people from different parts of west and west central Africa found themselves being thrown together on a particular estate, it could take them a while to find a language, often their own version of English, that enabled them to communicate with one another. But it would take more than being able to communicate with other people on the plantation to foster a successful rebellion.

Tobacco and rice plantations tended to be at some miles from one another, and this meant that slaves also had to contend with the problem of communicating and coordinating their planned uprising over significant distances. Owners and colonial governments alike were determined to make it as difficult as they possibly could for slaves on different plantations to communicate with one another. They did this, for example, by introducing a pass system, which meant that slaves had to have the written permission of their owner or overseer before they could leave their plantations. Any white person was authorized to stop any black person and ask to see their pass. If a pass was not produced, the white person was allowed to punish the slave.

Many planters thought that slaves sent messages to one another across several miles by playing drums, something they unsuccessfully tried to stamp out. By the late seventeenth century, they knew that slaves from neighboring plantations were gathering together, usually at night, supposedly for various religious purposes, but mainly for burying their dead. These nighttime burials may have been the continuation of a common west African practice, or because owners were unwilling to allow slaves time off work to conduct funerals. But whatever the truth of the matter, owners preferred to believe that the real reason for these nighttime meetings was to plot rebellion, and no doubt this was sometimes the case.

Yet even if rebellions were being hatched, in order to stand any realistic chance of success they had to surmount two major obstacles. First, owners tried to maintain their security by pursuing a policy of divide and rule. They offered various incentives, including freedom from bondage, to those within the slave community who were willing to betray conspiracies. And they were able to find those who were willing to place their self-interest above that of their compatriots. Second, even if they managed to avoid detection or betrayal during the planning stages of their projected uprising, enslaved rebels knew that they would be confronted by the superior weaponry, as well as by the well-trained militias, that were readily available to white authorities. Rebels might be able to lay their hands on a few guns but, unless they could, they would be armed only with the agricultural tools they worked with. Hoes, shovels, and axes were poor substitutes for the arms that they would be confronted by.

A successful rebellion, and one that could have produced a revolutionary change, might have been achieved had slaves been able to enlist the support of lower-class white people. Indentured servants, landless whites, and blacks who were in the process of being enslaved had fought together during Bacon's Rebellion in Virginia in 1676, and the possibility that this might happen again, perhaps even on a larger scale, was never completely absent from the minds of planters. Yet it was something that did not happen during the remainder of the colonial period. True, relations between poor whites and slaves were not always or necessarily hostile, but by and large planters succeeded in driving a wedge between them. They did this in part through the continuing use of a language that degraded people of African descent. African peoples were described as beastly and barbaric, as being barely human, and therefore suitable only for enslavement. The worth and superiority of Europeans, of those with white skin, whatever their social class, was constantly emphasized. Another, more practical, way in which planters drew in underclass whites in defense of their interests was the legal requirement that they serve regularly in slave patrols and urban watches.

The only other way in which a successful rebellion or revolution might have been achieved was with help from foreign nations. The European struggle for supremacy in North America held out the hope that such assistance might be forthcoming from Britain's two main imperial rivals, France and Spain, and to some extent it was. As war erupted in the late seventeenth century between France and Britain in the New England region, New Englanders feared that the French would use slaves as part of their war effort. They thought that slaves would be encouraged to run away and join the French. British colonists tightened controls, and some thought that the dangerous circumstances demanded a limitation on the number of slaves imported into New England. Some slaves did escape to the French, but they never assumed a significant role in that country's continuing military campaigns against the British. Forty years later it would be a very different story indeed when Spain and Britain went to war on the southern frontier.

Spain and England had long disputed the ownership of the territory that stretched between Virginia and Florida, but matters came to a head during the 1730s. This was at a time when South Carolina's rice revolution was well underway and the colony was becoming of ever-increasing economic value to Britain. At all costs, the British government believed, South Carolina had to be defended.

In 1733, the British, under the leadership of General James Oglethorpe, created a new colony, Georgia. Its purpose was mainly, but not exclusively, to protect South Carolina from falling to a Spanish attack. Spain was determined to get rid of this new settlement and thought that the growing number of slaves in South Carolina would be more than willing to help them do so. The Spanish offered freedom to any slaves who were willing to run away from their English owners and able to make their way to the Spanish fort of St. Augustine, located on the northeastern coast of Florida. Once they arrived, these enslaved men could choose to serve in the Spanish forces, which would wage war on the English settlers in Georgia and South Carolina. During the 1730s many slaves took advantage of this offer, and with the support of the Spanish established themselves at a place called Fort Moosa, close to St. Augustine.

It was this prospect of freedom that sparked one of the major slave uprisings of the colonial period, the 1739 Stono Rebellion. William Bull, the lieutenant governor of South Carolina, was taking a leisurely ride in the countryside one morning when he got the shock of his life: Marching toward him was a party of around fifty armed slaves heading in a southerly direction. Bull rushed off to get help, and once that help arrived the outcome was a foregone conclusion. Despite the resistance they put up, the poorly armed rebels were quickly killed by the well-armed whites that Bull had managed to muster. Without any pretence of a trial, many of the rebels who were taken alive were summarily executed, and their heads placed on poles by the roadside as a grisly reminder to passers by. To slaves they provided an unmistakable example of the price they would pay for rebellion. To whites they suggested the ever-present possibility of rebellion and the need for them to be always on their guard.

The context was very different, but similar difficulties awaited those slaves who were involved in the two other major uprisings that took place in the mainland colonies before the American Revolution. In 1712, and again in 1741, there were uprisings, not in the southern mainland, but in New York City. As in South Carolina, once they had got over their initial shock, and organized themselves, the New York authorities were able to put down these revolts with comparative ease. Like the planter-politicians of South Carolina, they took their bloody vengeance on those they thought, or knew, to have been the ringleaders.

Everywhere in the mainland, slaves were fully aware of the difficulties involved in organizing rebellion on any significant scale, and the terrible price that awaited them should they fail. They also knew that they would have to pay exactly the same price for any individual acts of physical violence they directed toward their owners or toward any white person. Yet sometimes out of sheer rage and frustration, sometimes in order to try and protect themselves against white violence, and sometimes as a prelude to escape, slaves were responsible for a wide range of physical attacks on whites, especially on their owners and their owners' families. Such uncoordinated attacks were not going to bring about the collapse of slavery anywhere in the mainland, but particularly in the plantation colonies of the South owners could never rule out the possibility of being assaulted, or murdered, by those they held in bondage.

Owners could never be entirely certain that their household slaves would not poison them, and sometimes that happened. There were two main ways in which slaves could acquire poisons. The first, which often reflected knowledge brought directly from Africa, involved using various herbs and plants, the same knowledge that was also used in the manufacture of a range of herbal medicines. The second way was by obtaining a poison such as arsenic. This was not always as difficult as it might seem, given that on many plantations poison was laid to get rid of rats and other vermin. Southern governments passed laws that tried to prevent slaves from getting their hands on any poisonous substances, but these were far from watertight. In fact, despite these laws, in places such as Virginia and South Carolina, owners were so paranoid about the possibility of being poisoned by their slaves, be it by herbs or by arsenic and the like, that what might well have been natural deaths from ailments such as gastroenteritis were blamed on slaves, who could find themselves on trial for their lives.

Arson, being burned alive in their beds, was something else that owners feared as well, and slaves were blamed for many unexplained fires. Sometimes, slaves were responsible for deliberately or accidentally burning down a house or another building, but on other occasions they were not. As with poisoning, it was what the owner, or the colonial authorities, believed that was the important thing. In the minds of their owners, slaves were the prime suspects when something like a barn burned down.

If charged with poisoning or arson, slaves were usually tried before a court consisting of local slave owners. Even if innocent, those found guilty of either of these offences were executed, always in public. Most were hanged, but in some cases they were burned alive. This happened to an unnamed enslaved woman in Savannah, Georgia, on the eve of the American Revolution. She confessed to having attempted to poison her owner and his wife with arsenic, and after a short trial she was condemned to be burned alive on Savannah Common.

Other slaves vented their anger not on their owners or overseers, but on their owners' property. Tools might be lost or destroyed and farm animals killed or wounded by slaves, actions that owners often interpreted not as resistance but as indicative of the natural foolishness and incompetence of Africans. In many ways, these kinds of activities reinforced the owners' belief in the inferiority of Africans and their suitability for enslavement.

Much the same was true of another kind of slave behavior that owners frequently complained about, and that was theft. Southern planters believed that, if given the chance, there was nothing that slaves would not make off with. If anything—from chickens and hogs to their clothes and household utensils—went missing then, rightly or wrongly, slaves were usually the first to be suspected. Sometimes, and with good reason, slaves did steal. For example, they pilfered foodstuffs in order to supplement the stingy and unvarying diets provided by their owners. Sometimes they took items of clothing to supplement their well-worn working clothes. As their owners suspected, whenever and wherever they could they traded or sold some of the things they had purloined—things that might not be of immediate practical use to them—for the things they needed or wanted. Given the willingness of enslaved people to trade with one another, and that of some whites to trade with slaves, there was little that either owners or the white authorities could do about this.

However much they might have wanted to, and been tempted to, not every slave committed physically violent acts against his or her owners and the owner's property, and not every slave stole from his or her owners on a regular basis. But in one way or another, all slaves tried the best they could to assert their personalities and their individuality and to reclaim their dignity as human beings. They did this in various, and often in highly imaginative, ways. For example, they used their bodies to assert their individuality and their personality. The clothing slaves wore when they were not at work, the accessories such as scarves and earrings that they managed to acquire, and the ways in which they styled their hair, were all highly visible statements both to their owners and to each other of their individualism and self-pride. In the societies of early America, where someone's social rank and prestige was immediately visible by the clothing he or she wore, and were expected to wear, the sight of enslaved people wearing clothing as good as, if not better, than that of some whites was deeply disturbing. In mid-eighteenth-century South Carolina, for example, there were complaints that some slaves, especially in Charleston, were able to dress themselves better than their owners and demands were made that laws be enacted to prevent this from happening. In practice, nothing was done and, through their own initiative and by their own efforts, enslaved people continued to express themselves and their aspirations through the clothing they chose to wear.

Collectively, within their families, and sometimes through their religious rituals that brought them into contact with nonfamily members, slaves sought to reclaim something else that their colonial owners tried to strip from them: their history, their west and west central African pasts. Of course, what owners could not steal from slaves were their individual and collective memories of those pasts to which, either during their lifetimes or after their deaths, they hoped and believed they would return. Those pasts found expression in the continuation of African religious beliefs and rituals, in the ways in which enslaved parents named their children, and in the stories that were told in the slave quarters.

Everywhere, in the North as well as in the South, in the towns as well as in the countryside, slaves of both sexes and of all ages were engaged in continual negotiations with their owners, and in varying degrees with other whites, not simply to assert their individuality or to bring about an immediate end to their bondage, but also to claim certain rights and certain kinds of protection while they remained enslaved. These negotiations took various forms, and they took place in different arenas. Sometimes, slaves were able to exploit the Christian conscience of their owners in order to avoid a whipping or being sold apart from their families. In the workplace slaves ran the risk of punishment, sometimes brutal physical punishment, by refusing to work as hard as their owners demanded. They also refused to work in what they claimed as their own time, notably on Sundays, unless they received some reward for their extra labor. This reward sometimes came in form of material goods, such as food or clothing, and sometimes owners were so desperate to get this extra work from their slaves that they were willing to pay them in cash.

These were all negotiations in which gender played a significant part. Enslaved women were able to use their bodies in ways in which enslaved men simply could not. Sometimes, for example, slave women pretended to be pregnant and were able to persuade their owners either to give them lighter work or to remove them from the workforce altogether until their babies were born. In some cases, the alleged pregnancy went on for more than nine months before the owners concerned realized that they had been duped. Usually, these women paid a heavy physical price, in the shape of a whipping, when their subterfuge was discovered.

The most widespread way in which slaves of both sexes asserted themselves was by running away. This might be in the hope of securing their permanent freedom from bondage or for other reasons. As with other acts of self-assertion, running away was unlikely to topple the institution of slavery, but it was a major economic irritant and source of great concern to owners as well as to colonial authorities. For owners it meant the loss, perhaps permanent, perhaps temporary, of valuable workers and valuable pieces of property. It also meant something else: Potentially, a slave who was not under the immediate authority of an owner, or other whites, was a most dangerous person.

We can never know for certain how many enslaved people ran away during the colonial period, where they headed for, or how successful they were in achieving their objectives. One of our best sources of evidence comes in the shape of the advertisements for enslaved runaways that were placed in colonial newspapers by owners seeking the return of their slaves beginning in the 1730s. Not every slave who ran away was advertised in this way; some were captured or returned voluntarily before their owners resorted to an advertisement. But the hundreds of advertisements that were placed in newspapers published in towns as far apart as Boston and Savannah provide a wealth of information about fugitives. Given that they were seeking the return of their valuable property and workers, most owners provided as accurate descriptions as they could of those who had taken flight. Advertisements often included details of slaves' ages, occupation, linguistic skills, the clothing they wore when they ran away, any possessions they took with them, and their likely destination.

These advertisements also reveal that in every colony, and in town and countryside alike, far more men than women took flight. This did not mean that enslaved women were afraid to run away, but when compared with men they were at a disadvantage. For example, there is a lot of evidence to suggest that enslaved mothers were less likely to run away if this meant abandoning their babies and young children. Some mothers did take flight with their children, but this could make their lives extremely difficult while they were on the run.

According to their owners, slaves ran away for several reasons and to many different destinations. Owners made no secret of the fact that one of the most common reasons why slaves took flight was in an attempt to be reunited with loved ones from whom they had been forcibly separated. But even if runaways did find their loved ones, the chances were that theirs would be a relatively brief reunion. They might be hidden out for a while, but there was always the very real possibility of being discovered. Being discovered meant being returned to the owner and, in all probability, being whipped and possibly made to wear heavy leg or neck irons in order to prevent another escape. If nothing else, the published advertisements testify to the hundreds of enslaved people who thought that these were risks well worth running, to the strong bonds of love and affection that characterized enslaved families.

There were other enslaved people who ran away in search of freedom, either their permanent freedom from slavery or quasi-independence in one of the colonial towns. The destinations of those who sought their permanent liberation varied, but it is evident that by no means had slaves entirely given up the hope of being able to return to Africa. On the eve of the American Revolution, for example, a group of newly enslaved African people made their way down the Savannah River, heading for the open sea in a canoe. Their owner was convinced that they were trying to make their way to Africa. There is no record of how far these people got or of what eventually happened to them.

Other slaves also saw the sea as a possible means of escape and they made their way to one of the port towns. They hoped to be able to persuade a ship's captain or crew to take them on board. They took their chances in whichever destination they eventually found themselves. Their escape route was also gendered. Enslaved men might be able to convince the ship's captain that they were not only free but also experienced sailors, an option that was closed to female slaves. If they hoped to escape by sea, they had to be willing to resort to other tactics, including possibly trading sexual favors, in order to persuade the captain or crew to take them on board.

Many runaways remained in the port towns. This was because they were still waiting for an opportunity to escape by sea or because they did not wish to completely abandon their families and friends. With varying degrees of success, and often with the help of family members and friends, they were able to blend in with the black urban crowd. Many managed to support themselves by hiring out their labor to white employers, who were willing to turn a blind eye to the law if it meant that they could obtain cheap workers. How long such runaways managed to evade recapture was a matter of chance. It depended upon the luck of not being betrayed for a reward or being stopped by the urban watch. If challenged by a white person it might also depend upon the ability of being able to talk one's way out of trouble.

Other slaves also stayed on land, but headed for the frontier regions of the mainland in order to try to put as much distance as they could between themselves and their former owners. Some simply disappeared to live out their lives in the American wilderness, never to be heard of again, while others joined Native American peoples. Sometimes they lived and intermarried with the Native Americans; sometimes, often after several years, their return was demanded in the treaties between these Native Americans and the English, and they found themselves back in captivity.

The infrequency and failure of organized slave rebellions in the mainland colonies should not be taken as evidence that slaves were cowed into unthinking and uncritical acceptance of the degraded lives and the perpetual bondage that their owners and white society generally sought to impose upon them. From the early seventeenth century to the time of the American Revolution, the chances of successful rebellion, let alone a revolutionary overthrow of the institution of slavery, were so slim as to be virtually nonexistent. Yet during the 1760s and 1770s, as relations between Britain and the mainland colonies deteriorated to the point of war, the overthrow of slavery was a distinct possibility. For the first time, the institution of slavery came under heavy assault by white critics, on both sides of the Atlantic. That assault, together with a war that politically divided the colonists, seemed to offer slaves the best chance yet of securing their permanent freedom from bondage.

# CHAPTER SEVEN

∿

# Critiques and Defenses of Slavery

For most of the seventeenth century, the enslavement of African peoples in every part of the North American mainland under British control, including New Netherland, went unquestioned and uncontested, both in the Old World and in the New. Successive British monarchs and governments, who secured revenues from colonial trade, particularly with the plantation colonies, displayed virtually no interest in the fate of those shipped to the mainland as well as to the sugar islands of the British Caribbean in ever-increasing numbers by the 1680s and 1690s.

The British authorities did not intervene in the political processes that resulted in colonial governments enacting legislation that, by the end of the seventeenth century, had made the enslavement of Africans the norm everywhere in the North American mainland. Neither did the London-based Anglican hierarchy raise any objections to slavery on purely religious grounds. Beginning in the mid-seventeenth century onward, the Anglican Church held tenaciously to the opinion that there was absolutely nothing in Christian doctrine to prevent one Christian from holding another Christian in perpetual bondage. Finally, British consumers displayed no concern about the cruelly exploitative labor systems that supplied them with the tobacco and sugar they were buying in ever-increasing amounts.

It was not until 1688 that a small community of Dutch Quakers who had settled just outside Philadelphia, in Germantown, voiced the first recorded semipublic questioning of the enslavement of Africans in British America. Until this point, both in Europe and in North America, the Quakers had adopted a position on the relationship between Christianity and bondage that was identical to that of the Anglican Church. They held that slaveholding was not sinful and that the scriptures permitted one Christian to hold another Christian as a slave. However, Quakers urged Christian masters and mistresses to attend to both the spiritual and the material needs of their slaves, who, in the same way as their children, were totally dependent upon them. Provided that Quakers took these duties seriously, slavery would be permitted in William Penn's "Holy Experiment," the colony of Pennsylvania.

It was this interpretation of the scriptures that the Germantown Quakers queried, and that they requested their coreligionists to consider in their quarterly and yearly meetings. Their request greatly embarrassed prominent Quakers in Philadelphia, many of whom were slaveholders and some of whom were already getting involved both in the slave trade and in the carrying of goods, such as sugar, that were produced by slaves elsewhere in the Americas. The Germantown Petition was shelved, and no action was taken. But even so, this petition marked the beginning of what would prove to be one of the most significant, and most influential, of all the eighteenth-century critiques of slavery and the transatlantic slave trade. By the mid-eighteenth century, the Bible became one of the main weapons employed by both sides in the growing battle over the legitimacy of slavery and the slave trade.

The Germantown Petition did not provoke a long-lived dispute among the Quakers of the Middle Atlantic colonies, and much the same was true of a public argument that took place twelve years later in Massachusetts. In 1700, at a time when the number of slaves being brought to New England was on the increase, Massachusetts' Judge Samuel Sewell published a pamphlet entitled *The Selling of Joseph*, in which he condemned the institution of slavery, referring to it as being equivalent to man stealing. Judge John Saffin, who had recently fallen out with Sewell, and who was also a slave owner, quickly put pen to paper in an attempt to refute Sewell's antislavery arguments. In *A Brief and Candid Answer to a Late Printed Sheet, Entitled,* The Selling of Joseph, a pamphlet he published a year later, Saffin claimed that the Old Testament allowed the holding of slaves. He also suggested that Africans were racially inferior to Europeans and that for this reason they were ineligible to enjoy the rights and liberties claimed by Europeans.

Between them, Sewell and Saffin raised most of the issues that would come to dominate the intense debate about the institution of slavery and the transatlantic slave trade that got underway during the 1760s and 1770s. In the short term, however, their quarrel amounted to a localized storm in a teacup. It did not prompt an ongoing debate, even in Massachusetts, let alone elsewhere in the mainland colonies, about the rightness or wrongness of slavery and the slave trade.

The first extensive argument about the institution of slavery occurred during the 1730s and 1740s, not in the Middle Atlantic or New England colonies but in the southern mainland. It was sparked by the founding of Georgia in 1733, the last British colony to be settled on the North American mainland. General James Oglethorpe and the other British founders of Georgia—a mixture of merchants, Anglican churchmen, and politicians—intended this new colony to serve three main functions. It was to act as a military buffer between South Carolina and Spanish Florida, offer unemployed and unemployable British people opportunities for social and economic advancement, and provide Britain with a range of valuable Mediterranean-type goods such as silk. Each of these objectives persuaded Georgia's founders, known as the Trustees, that slavery would not only be unnecessary in their colony but also a positive danger to its very survival.

The Trustees argued that, unlike rice cultivation, silk production did not require an enslaved African workforce. Moreover, they realized that, with or without Spanish encouragement, any slaves brought to Georgia would seize every opportunity that presented itself to make a bid for their freedom. Thus, they could be a source of constant danger to the colony's white settlers. When, in 1735, the Trustees persuaded the British Parliament to pass a law that prohibited slavery in Georgia, there was no serious opposition to it in Britain, but neither was it applauded as a move toward the ultimate abolition of slavery and the transatlantic slave trade.

In Georgia, though, it was a very different matter. Almost immediately, a growing number of settlers began to challenge the prohibition and, in the process, they became the first British American colonists who argued a case in favor of the institution of slavery out of personal interest. For the next fifteen years, together with their South Carolinian allies, who were keen to expand their slave-based rice economy into the Georgia lowcountry, they bombarded the Trustees with letters, pamphlets, and petitions stating their reasons for permitting slavery in the colony. With one notable exception, most of the arguments foreshadowed the proslavery arguments that would be used by the planter-politicians of Georgia and South Carolina during the era of the American Revolution.

Religion, or more specifically the long-standing question as to the exact relationship between Christianity and slavery, played only a minor part in the argument that raged during the late 1730s and 1740s about whether or not slavery should be introduced to Georgia. Religion was seldom used either to justify or to defend a change in the Trustees' policy. Instead, the supporters focused primarily on the practical matter of the comparative economic advantages and disadvantages of slavery as a labor system in the context of the lowcountry's physical environment. The Trustees and their few supporters in Georgia were convinced that Europeans could live and work productively in this part of the world without slaves. Their opponents claimed that this was utterly impossible, and that in terms of their productivity and profitability, enslaved Africans were superior to any other workers. In their opinion, if Georgia was ever to prosper then it had to follow the example of South Carolina.

By the late 1740s the aggressive campaign waged by the Trustees' opponents had succeeded and, in 1750, the British Parliament passed a law that permitted slavery in Georgia. During the next twenty-five years, not least because of the migration of South Carolina planters and their slaves across the Savannah River, lowcountry Georgia developed a slave-based rice economy that was virtually identical to that of neighboring South Carolina. And, as in South Carolina, rice planters turned to the transatlantic slave trade for the workers they needed to expand their operations. Between 1750 and 1775, the black slave population of Georgia grew from less than 200 to around 16,000, and this was almost entirely due to the slave trade. By the mid-1750s it was already as if the earlier debate about the pros and cons of allowing slavery in Georgia had never taken place. That debate did not give rise to an enduring antislavery sentiment in the colony. Georgia planters were now as deeply committed to the institution of slavery, both as an economic system and as a means of trying to secure racial control, as were their neighbors in South Carolina.

The fifteen-year-long transatlantic, public debate about the future of Georgia did not spark a wide-ranging discussion about either the transatlantic slave trade or the institution of slavery elsewhere in British America. On neither side of the Atlantic did those discussions bring into existence anything resembling a coherent antislavery movement. Yet during the 1740s and 1750s, not in Georgia but further north, in the Middle Atlantic colonies, the seeds of such a movement, or movements, were in fact beginning to be sown.

The Germantown Petition of 1688 did not secure immediate widespread support among the Quaker communities of Pennsylvania and New Jersey, but it was important in helping to persuade a very small minority of Quakers of the sinfulness and injustice of both the slave trade and slaveholding. During the first forty years of the eighteenth century, two Quakers in particular, Ralph Sandiford and Benjamin Lay, were mainly responsible for keeping the antislavery message alive in the Middle Atlantic colonies. However, they were not very successful in converting other Quakers to their cause.

In Lay's case, this was almost certainly due to what many of his Quaker contemporaries thought of as his eccentric behavior. For a while he lived in a cave, and refused to use sugar, which, he insisted, had been made from and with the blood of slaves, his fellow human beings. On another occasion, he doused a Quaker meeting with what purported to be blood, accusing those present of compromising their pacifist principles by their involvement in the slave trade. That trade, he insisted, both stemmed from and encouraged wars in Africa. Influential Quakers dismissed Lay as an eccentric and continued to believe that, provided that they fulfilled their duties as Christian masters and mistresses, there was absolutely nothing at all wrong in holding or trading in slaves. If any one person is to be credited with changing their minds, and forcing antislavery sentiments into the mainstream of Quaker thought, then it was John Woolman.

John Woolman lived in New Jersey, where he worked as an assistant in a general store. One of his jobs was to write documents of various kinds, including bills of sale, for people who were unable to do so for themselves. According to his own account, for most of the time Woolman gave little thought to what he was being asked to write, until one day in 1743. After he had finished writing a document for one of his customers, it suddenly dawned on him what he had just done: He had written out a bill of sale for an enslaved woman; he had been complicit in selling one human being to another. From this point on, John Woolman was a driven man, a tortured soul. The dreadfulness, the sinfulness, of what he had done would haunt him for the rest of his life. He sought redemption and divine forgiveness in the only way he knew, by trying to bring about an end to all colonial and British involvement in slavery and the transatlantic slave trade.

For the remainder of his life, Woolman traveled extensively in the mainland colonies spreading his antislavery message. However, apart from his 1744 *Journal*, in which he set out his antislavery arguments, he published virtually nothing. Religion, and more specifically Quaker notions of spiritual equality and brotherhood, was at the very heart of his assault on slavery and the slave trade. He insisted that nothing could eradicate the sinfulness of both these activities. In the eyes of God, Woolman argued, performing the role of the good Christian master or mistress was simply irrelevant. Trying to convert slaves to Christianity and tending to their bodily needs could not and would not save Christian slave owners from divine punishment, either in this world or in the next.

John Woolman probably knew of Benjamin Lay, and might well have seen him in action, and he went about his antislavery business in a much more prudent manner. His antislavery strategy was based on calm, but firm, reasoned argument. But Woolman's methods might have been just as unsuccessful as those favored by Benjamin Lay had it not been for one thing: the crisis that hit the colony of Pennsylvania during the early 1750s.

Tensions of one sort or another along Pennsylvania's western border intensified during the 1740s and, even before the Seven Years' War between Britain, France, and Spain broke out in the mid-1750s, they had reached boiling point. The Quaker-dominated government of Pennsylvania found itself under increasing pressure from two directions to abandon its pacifist principles. On the one hand, the mainly Presbyterian Scotch-Irish migrants who had settled in the frontier regions demanded that the colonial government provide them with the means to defend themselves against both Native Americans and the French, who were increasingly active in this part of the world. Simultaneously, the British government was requiring exactly the same thing of the Quakers.

Rather than compromise their pacifism, the Quakers gave up their posts in the Pennsylvania government. This prompted an intense amount of soul searching as to why the "Holy Experiment" of Pennsylvania that had been embarked upon in the 1680s had come to such an inglorious end. What had gone wrong? Why was God punishing them in this way? John Woolman and Anthony Benezet, another Quaker who by this time had become deeply committed to the cause of antislavery, had a ready answer: God was punishing the Quakers for the twin sins of slave trading and slaveholding. Only by abandoning these wicked activities could they hope for forgiveness and redemption. This was a message that appealed to a growing number of Quakers, and through the 1750s and 1760s antislavery began to emerge as a significant component of mainstream Quaker philosophy.

Woolman and Benezet, who became the movement's chief publicist, spearheaded an antislavery campaign that operated along several different fronts. Both men strenuously opposed slavery and the slave trade on religious grounds, but they also displayed a familiarity with other, essentially new, antislavery arguments that were beginning to emerge in British and continental European thought. In fact, like the Trustees of Georgia and some of their spokesmen, John Woolman went some way toward anticipating those arguments.

By the mid-eighteenth century, in France and Britain, Enlightenment thinkers such as Montesquieu, Voltaire, Hume, and Hutcheson were in the process of completely rethinking and redefining traditional notions of individual rights and liberties. Now, emphasis came to be attached to the idea of a cluster of natural rights to which all men were equally entitled, regardless of their ethnicity or their religious preferences. One of the main roles of government was to uphold those rights and either individually or collectively citizens could legitimately resist any tyrannical attempts to deny them their rights.

During the 1760s and 1770s the possible implications of these strands of Enlightenment thought for the institution of slavery became the subject of intense debate throughout the mainland colonies, and they were themes that John Woolman had already addressed in his *Journal*. Unless it was possible to establish that God had created Africans separately from mankind, which Woolman vehemently claimed it was not, then the humanity that they shared with Europeans fully entitled them to all the natural rights claimed by Europeans, including the right to personal freedom. But were Africans by nature the mental and intellectual equals of Europeans and, if so, did this necessarily disqualify them from full and equal participation in political society? Woolman argued that it was enslavement in America, and the complete denial of all educational opportunities, that was entirely responsible for generating the illusion of African inferiority.

Anthony Benezet tried to substantiate this argument by opening a school in Philadelphia in which black and white children were taught side by side. Benezet was quickly convinced that an equality of opportunity and access to education produced an equal spread of results. Black children, he argued, displayed exactly the same range of natural ability, and talents, as did their white counterparts.

Meanwhile, in Boston, a young enslaved woman named Phillis Wheatley was in the process of gaining a transatlantic reputation as a poet, and her achievements were seized upon by the critics of slavery as yet more evidence in support of their argument that those of African ancestry were just as mentally gifted as their European counterparts. Phillis had been born in the Senegal-Gambia region of west Africa, and in 1760 or 1761, when she was about seven years old, had been placed on a slave ship bound for the Americas. She was taken to Boston, where she was bought by a tailor named John Wheatley, who thought she could be trained to work as a personal maid for his wife. The Wheatleys helped Phillis to learn English, and within months they realized that she was an immensely gifted child.

Within fewer than two years after her arrival in Boston, at the age of nine or ten, Phillis was able to read the Bible, dipping into Greek and Latin clas-

**Phillis Wheatley**

Source: Phillis Wheatley, *Poems on Various Subjects, Religious and Moral* (London 1773). By permission of the Syndics of Cambrige University Library.

sics, and had an excellent grasp of geography and history. With the continuing encouragement of the Wheatleys, she was also beginning to write poetry.
She published her first poem in a Rhode Island newspaper in 1767, and six
years later thirty-nine of her poems were published in London, under the
title *Poems on Various Subjects, Religious and Moral*. Phillis Wheatley was a

sensation on both sides of the Atlantic, and one of her most significant achievements was to demonstrate the natural intellectual and mental abilities of Africans. As Benezet and Woolman argued, and as Phillis so clearly demonstrated, it was the complete denial of educational opportunities to enslaved people that had created the illusion of their mental and intellectual inferiority.

Another significant theme touched on by Woolman in his *Journal*, and one developed at greater length during the Revolutionary era, particularly by Adam Smith in his *Wealth of Nations*, published in 1776, concerned the economics of slavery. As the debate over the introduction of slavery into Georgia during the 1730s and 1740s had demonstrated, most people in the southern colonies still believed, as they had believed ever since the mid-seventeenth century, that slave labor was considerably more profitable than any other form of labor available to them. They had no doubt that their economic prosperity depended upon the continuing employment of slaves, but Woolman wondered whether this was in fact the case. In the process he raised another important issue: the social consequences of slavery.

The gist of Woolman's argument was that unlike indentured servants and free workers, slaves had absolutely no incentive to work, and certainly not to work hard, in the hope and expectation of thereby improving their lot in life. However hard they worked for their owners, slaves would not be rewarded with either their freedom or, for that matter, with greatly improved living conditions. There was only one way, Woolman concluded, that slaves could be made to work hard enough to satisfy their greedy owners, and that was by force, by the threat or application of brutal and unchristian physical punishments.

By the early 1760s, Woolman and Benezet realized that because of the commitment of many slave owners, mainly in the South but also further north, to the institution of slavery, and the depth of their racism, argument alone was unlikely to bring about either an immediate or a more gradual end to either the transatlantic slave trade or to slaveholding anywhere in the mainland colonies. These objectives, they had come to believe, could be achieved only by taking their case into the political arena through the organization of a concerted political campaign that would operate on both sides of the Atlantic. The institutional organization of the Quakers, their monthly, quarterly, and yearly meetings, provided them with the means of doing just that. What Woolman and Benezet hoped for, and what they set about planning, was a unified transatlantic campaign against slavery and the slave trade that would be spearheaded by colonial and British Quakers. The plan was for British Quakers to secure Parliamentary legislation that would outlaw slavery and the slave trade and for colonial Quakers to seek exactly the same thing from their local governments. In 1772, Woolman was in England discussing this Anglo-American strategy with English Quakers but, while on a visit to York, he contracted smallpox, from which he died.

With Woolman's untimely death, the antislavery campaign had lost one of its most eloquent and committed leaders. Anthony Benezet continued to publish antislavery tracts and promoted the cause, but within a year of Woolman's death, the struggle to close the slave trade and to abolish the institution of slavery in the mainland colonies was severely set back by the outbreak of war. As the war continued, colonial Quakers increasingly found themselves detested, and their antislavery campaign discredited, because of their pacifism and their almost universal refusal to take up arms and fight for either Britain or the American rebels.

By 1775, however, antislavery sentiments in the mainland American colonies were by no means confined to the Quakers. As Anthony Benezet readily admitted, it was the grounds upon which the American colonists came to challenge Britain's imperial policy after 1763, at the end of the Seven Years' War, rather than the efforts of the Quakers, that finally and irrevocably forced both the transatlantic slave trade and slaveholding into the forefront of the colonial political consciousness.

Increasingly, colonial opposition to such new British laws as the Stamp Act of 1765 emphasized the natural rights of the colonists, their rights to the same freedoms and liberties enjoyed in Britain itself, as well as their right to defend themselves against what they depicted as British attempts to tyrannize and enslave them. But as many people, both in the mainland colonies and in Britain, soon came to realize, or were made to realize, by advancing this line of argument the colonial leaders were laying themselves open to charges of blatant hypocrisy. After all, by this date black slaves accounted for around 20 percent of the total population of the mainland colonies. Significantly, about 80 percent of these slaves lived and worked in the colonies to the south of Pennsylvania. They were legally defined as pieces of property, and outside of New England, they were denied even the most basic human rights, let alone those being demanded by the colonists.

In towns as far apart as Savannah, Georgia, and Boston, Massachusetts, slaves heard for themselves the cries for liberty and freedom coming from the colonial crowds as they took to the streets to oppose British policy. Much to the alarm of their owners, these were cries that slaves began to take up— perhaps on behalf of the colonists but, far more worrying for owners, as part of their continuing struggle to secure a different kind of "liberty" and "freedom." In March 1770, colonial resistance to Britain took a more violent turn when five men who were part of a crowd taunting British troops were shot and killed in what quickly became known as the Boston Massacre. One of those who died was a black man called Crispus Attucks. Relatively little is known about Attucks. Some historians believe that he was an escaped slave who was working in Boston while trying to find a passage on a ship that would take him out of Massachusetts.

We do not know for sure whether Attucks was a committed opponent of British policy or whether he just found himself in the wrong place at the wrong time. But whatever his reason for being with the Boston crowd, Attucks was one of those gunned down by the British. He was the first black victim of the American Revolution and, almost overnight, became an enduring symbol of the sacrifices that the colonists, including African Americans, were willing to make in order to secure their freedom.

By the time that Crispus Attucks died, it was clear to most people in the mainland colonies that the future of slavery and the transatlantic slave trade could not be easily divorced from the practical political action, as well as the political ideology, being devised by the colonists in an attempt to secure a reversal of British policy. The significance that the colonists attached to trade boycotts as a means of forcing the British hand, and securing the concessions they sought, inevitably raised the question of the transatlantic slave trade: Ought that trade to be included in any embargo?

The southern colonies were divided on the issue. Virginia and Maryland's planter-politicians, whose slave population was growing as a result of natural increase, because of problems associated with tobacco cultivation in the tidewater were beginning to find that they had more slaves than they knew what to do with. Thus they were quite willing to close the transatlantic slave trade. After the War of Independence they would decide not to reopen it. It was a very different matter as far as South Carolina and Georgia were concerned. Their thriving rice economy was generating an intense demand for enslaved workers, but this was a demand that was not being met by natural reproduction; rice planters still needed the transatlantic slave trade. Although the political leaders of South Carolina and Georgia grudgingly agreed to close the slave trade as part of the Patriots' commercial warfare against Britain, they never contemplated its permanent closure. They were determined to reopen it as soon as they possibly could, and in fact they did so just as the War of Independence was drawing to a close.

In the realm of political ideology, as opposed to the world of practical politics, the colonists found that they could not easily ignore the charge that by continuing to sanction slaveholding they were acting hypocritically. For a growing number of their leaders, particularly in the New England and Middle Atlantic colonies, the answer was crystal clear. They argued that enslaved people of African descent had exactly the same human rights as did those of European ancestry and were entitled to exactly the same rights as those being sought by the colonists. But did they have the right, which the colonists were claiming by 1776, to take up arms, and rebel, if they continued to be denied their natural, human right to freedom? Few Patriots were willing to pursue this question, but one who did was the political radical Tom Paine.

Paine, who emigrated from England to Philadelphia on the eve of the American Revolution, and who galvanized opinion early in 1776 with the publication of his pamphlet *Common Sense*, was convinced that the logic of the colonists' demands for liberty and freedom required them to abolish the institution of slavery just as soon as they were in a position to do so. Paine believed not only that slavery should be abolished but also that enslaved people should be compensated by any newly independent state governments for the time they had been in bondage. Paine's proposal ran completely counter to the strategy of Benezet and others who suggested that slave owners might be persuaded to give up their slaves if they received some form of compensation for doing so. Paine's argument that if enslaved people were not given their freedom then they would have every right to rebel in order to secure that freedom failed to persuade Benezet and other white opponents of slavery. Not surprisingly, it was a proposition that horrified slave owners, particularly those in the southern colonies who lived in constant fear of slave rebellion.

In New England, with or without the help of white sympathizers, it was possible for slaves to peaceably test the validity of the assertion that they had just as much right to freedom as did the Patriots. In Massachusetts, they had never been deprived of their legal status as persons, and it was in that capacity that they petitioned both the colonial government and in courts of law for their freedom. Often they were successful. Even before the War of Independence, the first crucial steps had been taken toward the ending of slavery in Massachusetts, a process that would be completed by further lawsuits that were heard during the early 1780s. This was a process that was greatly helped by two things: slave owners were comparatively few in number and in no position to block the movement toward freedom. By the same token, the relatively small number of slaves in New England did not pose a particularly serious threat to either the economic or the physical well-being of the region's white inhabitants. But as those who were freed from slavery would quickly learn, their skin color, their African ancestry, meant that legal freedom would not necessarily gain them the rights, or the equality, enshrined in the Declaration of Independence.

It was a very different story further south. Nowhere did slaves have the right to approach either government or the law courts in search of their freedom. In their efforts to secure their freedom by legal or political means, they were dependent upon the inclinations and interests of their owners and other members of white society.

In the Middle Atlantic colonies, some owners were persuaded by Quaker arguments, revolutionary political ideology, or a combination of both these things, and freed their slaves immediately and unconditionally. Yet in New York, and even in the Quaker strongholds of Pennsylvania and New Jersey, slave owners were a sufficiently powerful group to be able to block unconditional or even gradual emancipation for many years after the War of Independence had ended. In fact, it would not be until the turn of the eighteenth century that New York and New Jersey finally passed laws providing for the gradual emancipation of slaves. There continued to be slaves in the so-called free Northern states well into the nineteenth century.

In Virginia on the eve of American independence, where enslaved people had no right of direct access to the white judicial system, the issue of slavery prompted a wide-ranging debate among that colony's most eminent planter-politicians, including Thomas Jefferson, James Monroe, and George Mason. A few planters, including Robert Carter, one of the largest slave owners in Virginia, did not need a debate to clarify their views. They had already determined that slaveholding was incompatible with Patriot ideology and had unconditionally manumitted their slaves. But for most leading planters the issue was by no means clear-cut. As far as most of them were concerned, the ending of slavery, whether gradually or over a period of several years, threatened them with many, and possibly insoluble, problems.

By the end of 1775, when war had already broken out in New England, a Proclamation issued by Lord Dunmore, who would be the last Royal Governor of Virginia, made it unthinkable for the colony's Patriots to voluntarily rid themselves of their slaves. To the absolute horror of white Virginians, Dunmore declared that any enslaved men who were owned by Patriots, and who were able to make their way to his headquarters, would be armed and employed, not behind the front line but as combat troops, as part of the British war effort. If they survived the war, they would be granted their freedom from bondage. This promise of freedom in exchange for military service was not based on any moral opposition to slavery but was a practical move designed to boost the manpower available to Britain in the southern mainland.

Enslaved people, including those who were owned by Loyalists, did not need asking twice if they would fight on Britain's side if that meant the chance of eventually securing their freedom. Here, it seemed, in the shape of Dunmore, was the outside assistance that would help them to secure their permanent escape from bondage. Within days, enslaved men, women, and children were flooding to join forces with Dunmore, and he was as good as

**John Murray, Fourth Earl of Dunmore**

Source: Sir Joshua Reynolds, *John Murray, 4th Earl of Dunmore.* By permission of the Scottish National Portrait Gallery.

his word. Approximately 500 enslaved men received military training and were recruited into an all-black regiment—commanded by white officers—that became known as Lord Dunmore's Ethiopian Regiment. The men in this Regiment wore sashes with an inscription that must have been both alarming and ironic to their Patriot owners: The wording on their sashes read "Liberty to Slaves." Slaves in Virginia, and very soon elsewhere in the South, were taking matters into their own hands. They were trying to claim their independence from slavery and the tyranny of their colonial owners and launched the initial stages of a black revolution.

The formation and active military service of the Ethiopian Regiment during the first few months of the war in Virginia, before it was forced to evacuate from the tidewater, did not remove the issue of slavery from the agenda of Virginia's Patriot politicians and lawmakers. When they met in the spring of 1776 to consider a Bill of Rights, in effect Virginia's declaration of independence from Britain, the first draft included a clause to the effect that all men were created equal and entitled to certain inalienable natural rights, including the right to liberty. The belief that such an assertion might be interpreted by slaves as well as white Virginians as meaning that slavery was about to end horrified elite planters, and they insisted that the draft be amended. The final version amended the original clause by stating that the rights referred to were applicable only to those who were "in a state of society." This neatly excluded Virginia's slaves who, according to that colony's political leaders, could not be said to be in a state of society.

Further south, in South Carolina and Georgia, there was no such debate, no such concern with the apparent inconsistency between the grounds upon which the Patriots were claiming their independence from Britain and the continuation of slavery. The attitude of the leading planter-politicians of the lowcountry was crystal clear. The enormous wealth that many of them enjoyed stemmed directly from their ownership of slaves. One of the main responsibilities of government, they argued, was that of protecting and guaranteeing the rights of its citizens, including their property rights. South Carolina and Georgia would not tolerate any outside interference, be it from Britain or from the other colonies that threatened their right to hold slaves.

Unlike some Virginians, including Thomas Jefferson, the South Carolinians and Georgians did not regard the institution of slavery as a "necessary evil," which at some point in the future, the distant future, might be brought to an end. In their opinion, far from being a necessary evil, slavery was a positive good and an institution that could readily be defended as such. The Bible, they argued, sanctioned slavery and the alleged natural inferiority of

African peoples qualified them for nothing better than a life of perpetual bondage. Such was the commitment of South Carolina and Georgia to the continuance of slavery that they made their entry into the war, and participation in nation building, conditional upon their demands being met by Northern politicians. Almost without exception, both during and immediately after the war, as the newly independent states embarked upon the process of national building, the South Carolinians and Georgians got the concessions they demanded.

With some justification, in 1775 it seemed to the colonists and also to those whom they held in perpetual bondage that the American Revolution would be about two kinds of slavery, two kinds of tyranny, and two kinds of freedom. The Patriots talked constantly about their enslavement by the British, about a tyrannical king, and the freedom to which they were entitled both as men and as Englishmen. "All men," they asserted in the Declaration of Independence, are "created equal" and thereby "entitled" to "certain inalienable rights," including "the right to life, liberty, and the pursuit of happiness." As many people, white and black, free and slave, were already wondering by 1776, in the event of an American victory would those inalienable rights be automatically extended to the slaves who made up just over a fifth of the American population? This question can be answered without the benefit of hindsight.

The political leadership of South Carolina and Georgia was unwavering in its commitment to the institution of slavery as an economic regime and as a means of trying to impose racial and social control. It was quite clear that, even as they were endorsing the Declaration of Independence, these planter-politicians would never voluntarily give up their slaves. Their counterparts in Virginia were more critical of slavery, mainly on the grounds of its corrupting influence on white society, but as of 1776 there was absolutely no indication that they would be willing to abandon it in the foreseeable future. Further north, particularly in New England, the outlook was considerably brighter and the obstacles to the ending of slavery far less insurmountable. Yet even if the Patriots were victorious, and of course that remained to be seen, there was no possibility whatsoever that northern politicians could force either the immediate or more gradual abolition of slavery upon reluctant and obstinate white southerners.

Slaves were perfectly well aware of these widely divergent attitudes on the part of the American revolutionaries. They may have hoped, but outside of New England they could scarcely have expected, that a Patriot victory would secure them their freedom from slavery or that the promises set out in the

Declaration of Independence would apply to them. But what, if anything, did the British have to offer them? Lord Dunmore's Proclamation implied that slaves who actively supported the British cause would secure their freedom; but there was no cast-iron guarantee that Dunmore and the British would triumph in the war and, even if they did, that they would keep their promise. The other possibility, given the deep political divisions within the white community, was to seize the chance to launch an armed black rebellion, a black revolution. Yet this too was a course of action that would be fraught with exactly the same difficulties that had always confronted would-be slave rebels. A black revolution would be immensely hard to organize and would stand little chance of success.

Other than the improbability of a successful black revolution, the only thing that was absolutely certain in 1776 was that the American War of Independence would be a war about the institution of slavery as well as about white freedom. This war and its outcome would determine the fate of all Americans, black and white, for the foreseeable future. What could not be foreseen in 1776 was that it would take almost another century, and another bloody war, to finally bring the institution of slavery to an end.

# Appendix

## Slaves Imported into Selected Mainland Colonies, 1619–1775

**Table 1.   Slaves Imported Into Virginia, 1619–1766**

| Years | From Africa | From Elsewhere | Total |
|---|---|---|---|
| 1619 | * | * | 21 |
| 1621–1623 | * | * | 3 |
| 1628 | * | * | 100 |
| 1635–1639 | * | * | 137 |
| 1642–1643 | * | * | 25 |
| 1649 | * | * | 17 |
| 1652 | * | * | 7 |
| 1662 | * | * | 80 |
| 1656 | * | * | 30 |
| 1670 | 150 | * | * |
| 1665 | * | * | 59 |
| 1678–1679 | 365 | * | * |
| 1685 | 190 | 1 | 191 |
| 1684 | 34 | * | * |
| 1687 | 120 | * | * |
| 1699 | * | * | 349 |
| 1700–1709 | 6,933 | * | * |
| 1721–1730 | 6,587 | 741 | * |
| 1710–1720 | 3,493 | 319 | * |
| 1731–1740 | 14,233 | 2,506 | 16,739 |
| 1741–1750 | 8,074 | 2,179 | 10,253 |
| 1751–1758 | 5,202 | 540 | 5,742 |
| 1760–1766 | 6,519 | 370 | 6,869 |

[* = data incomplete or unavailable]

**Table 2.  Slaves Imported Into New York, 1701–1764**

| Years | Total | From Africa | From other Continental Colonies | From Elsewhere |
|---|---|---|---|---|
| 1701–1710 | 302 | 77 | * | 225 |
| 1711–1720 | 1,334 | 549 | 11 | 774 |
| 1721–1730 | 1,580 | 176 | 74 | 1,330 |
| 1731–1739 | 1,208 | 233 | 72 | 903 |
| 1740–1748 | 142 | * | 13 | 129 |
| 1754 | 65 | 65 | * | * |
| 1763–1764 | 240 | 196 | * | 44 |

[* = data incomplete or unavailable]

**Table 3.  Slaves Imported Into Charleston, South Carolina, 1706–1775**

| Years | Total | From Africa | From Caribbean Ports | From N. American Ports | From Elsewhere |
|---|---|---|---|---|---|
| 1706–1710 | 337 | * | * | * | * |
| 1711–1716 | 972 | * | * | * | * |
| 1717–1719 | 1,726 | 1,007 | 611 | * | * |
| 1720–1721 | 766 | * | * | * | * |
| 1722 | 323 | * | 38 | * | * |
| 1723 | 436 | 192 | 38 | * | * |
| 1724 | 800 | 763 | 35 | 2 | * |
| 1725–1726 | 2,184 | * | * | * | * |
| 1727 | 652 | 610 | 42 | * | * |
| 1731–1740 | 17,323 | 16,280 | 998 | 39 | 6 |
| 1741–1750 | 1,562 | 1,356 | 205 | 1 | * |
| 1751–1760 | 18,839 | 16,035 | 2,764 | 40 | * |
| 1761–1770 | 18,705 | 15,154 | 3,410 | 138 | 3 |
| 1771–1775 | 19,215 | 15,872 | 3,075 | 259 | 9 |

[* = data incomplete or unavailable]

**Table 4. Slaves Imported Into Georgia, 1755–1771**

| Brought From | Number | % African imports | % all imports |
|---|---|---|---|
| **Africa** | | | |
| Gambia | 1,000 | 40 | 23 |
| Sierra Leone | 387 | 15 | 9 |
| Gambia & Sierra Leone | 154 | 6 | 3 |
| 'Rice Coast' (West Africa) | 340 | 14 | 8 |
| 'Grain Coast' (West Africa) | 130 | 5 | 3 |
| Angola | 250 | 10 | 6 |
| 'Africa' | 148 | 6 | 3 |
| Senegal | 78 | 3 | 2 |
| **Total** | **2,487** | | **57** |

| | Number | % Caribbean imports | % all imports |
|---|---|---|---|
| **Caribbean Islands** | | | |
| St. Christopher's/St.Kitts | 545 | 34 | 13 |
| Jamaica | 405 | 25 | 9 |
| Barbados | 147 | 9 | 3 |
| Montserrat | 136 | 8 | 3 |
| Curacao | 91 | 6 | 2 |
| St. Croix | 76 | 5 | 2 |
| Grenada | 75 | 5 | 2 |
| Antigua | 45 | 3 | 1 |
| Tortola | 28 | 2 | 1 |
| St. Vincent | 15 | 1 | 0.3 |
| St. Eustasius | 14 | 1 | 0.3 |
| Other Caribbean islands | 25 | 1 | 1 |
| **Total** | **1,612** | | **37.5** |

| | Number | % Mainland imports | % all imports |
|---|---|---|---|
| **Mainland colonies** | | | |
| South Carolina | 174 | 90 | 4 |
| New York/Rhode Island | 20 | 10 | 0.4 |
| **Total** | **194** | | **4.5** |
| **TOTAL** | **4,293** | | |

*Sources (for tables 1–4)*: United States Bureau of the Census, *Historical Statistics of the United States Colonial Times To 1970* 2 vols. (White Plains, New York, reprint, 1989); Elizabeth Donnan, ed. *Documents Illustrative of the History of the Slave Trade to America* 4 vols. (Washington, D.C., 1930–1935)

# The Enslaved Population of Selected Colonies
# in 1770, on the Eve of the American Revolution

Table 5.  The Enslaved Population of Selected Colonies in 1770

|  | Black Population | as % of Colonial Population |
|---|---|---|
| Virginia | 187,600 | 42 |
| Maryland | 63,818 | 32 |
| North Carolina | 69,600 | 35 |
| South Carolina | 75,178 | 61 |
| Georgia | 15,000 | 45 |
| New York | 19,062 | 12 |
| New Jersey | 8,220 | 7 |
| Pennsylvania | 5,561 | 2 |
| Rhode Island | 3,761 | 6 |
| Massachusetts | 4,754 | 2 |

Sources: United States Bureau of the Census, *Historical Statistics of the United States Colonial Times To 1970* 2 vols. (White Plains, New York, reprint, 1989); E. B. Greene and V. D. Harrington, *American Population Before The Federal Census of 1790* (New York, 1932); Robert V. Wells, *The Population of the British Colonies in America before 1776* (Princeton University Press, 1975).

# Documents

## 1. The Introduction and Consolidation of Slavery in The Mainland Colonies

### a. Slavery Permitted in Massachusetts, 1641

Extract from: *The Book of the General Lawes and Libertyes Concerning the inhabitants of Massachusetts.*

*In this document, which listed the rights and liberties of the Massachusetts settlers, the Puritans used traditional European arguments to justify bondage. They made no reference to the race or ethnicity of those who could be legitimately enslaved.*

[T]here shall never be any bond-slavery, villenage or captivitie amongst us; unless it be lawfull captives, taken in just warrs, and such strangers as willingly sell themselves, or are solde to us: and such shall have the libertyes and christian usages which the law of God established in Israell concerning such persons doth morally require, provided, this exempts none from servitude who shall be judged thereto by Authoritie. [1641]

### b. Growing Distinctions between Black and White in Seventeenth-Century Virginia

Extracts from: W. W. Hening, ed., *The Statutes at Large: Being a Collection of All the Laws of Virginia, from the First Session of the Legislature in the Year 1619* (1809–1823).

*These extracts from the seventeenth-century laws of Virginia show the growing trend toward a legal status that was based on supposed racial difference. By the middle years of the century Africans were being described as property rather than as persons and children inherited the legal status of their mothers. Conversion to Christianity offered no protection against enslavement.*

1630: Hugh Davis to be soundly whipped, before an assembly of Negroes and others for abusing himself to the dishonour of God and shame of Christians, by defiling his body in lying with a negro; which fault he has to acknowledge next Sabbath day.

1639: All persons except negroes to be provided with arms and ammunition or be fined at the pleasure of the Governor and Council.

1662: Whereas some doubts have arisen whether children got by an Englishman upon a negro woman should be slave or free, Be it therefore enacted and declared by this present grand assembly, that all children born in this country shall be held bond or free only according to the condition of the mother, And that if any Christian shall commit fornication with a negro man or woman, he or she so offending shall pay double the fines imposed by the former act.

1667: Whereas some doubts have risen whether children that are slaves by birth, and by the charity and piety of their owners made partakers of the blessed sacrament of baptism, should by virtue of their baptism be made free; It is enacted and declared by this grand assembly . . . that the conferring of baptism doth not alter the condition of the person as to his bondage or freedom.

1669: Be it enacted and declared by this grand assembly, if any slave resist his master (or other by his masters order correcting him) and by the extremity of the correction should chance to die, that his death shall not be accounted felony, but the master (or that other person appointed by the master to punish him) be acquit from molestation, since it cannot be presumed that prepensed malice (which alone makes murder felony) should induce any man to destroy his own property.

1680: Whereas the frequent meeting of considerable numbers of negro slaves under pretence of feasts and burials is judged of dangerous consequence, for prevention whereof for the future, Be it enacted . . . that it shall not be lawful for any negro or other slave to carry or arm himself with any club, staff, gun, sword or any other weapon of defence or offence, nor to go or depart from his masters ground without a certificate from his master, mistress, or overseer and such permission not to be granted but upon particular and necessary occasions; and every negro or slave so offending not having a certificate . . . shall [receive] twenty lashes on his bare back well laid on . . . And it is further enacted . . . that if any negro or other slave shall presume to lift his hand against any Christian, shall for every such offence . . . receive thirty lashes on his back well laid on.

1682: It is enacted that all servants . . . which shall be imported into this country either by sea or by land, whether Negroes, Moors, mulattoes or Indians who and whose parentage and native countries are not Christian at the time of their first purchase by some Christian . . . are hereby judged, deemed and taken to be slaves to all intents and purposes any law, usage, or custom to the contrary notwithstanding.

1705: [A]ll negro, mulatto, and Indian slaves . . . within this dominion, shall be held, taken, and adjudged, to be real estate (and not chattels) and shall descend unto the heirs and widows of persons departing this life, according to the manner and custom of land of inheritance, held in fee simple.

### c. Slavery Permitted in South Carolina, 1669

Extract from: *The Fundamental Constitutions of Carolina, 1669.*

*In 1669 the English founders of South Carolina drew up a constitution for the colony. In order to attract migrants from the British West Indies they sanctioned black slavery.*

Every freeman of Carolina shall have absolute power and authority over his negro slaves, of what opinion or religion soever.

## 2. The Transatlantic Slave Trade

### a. Capture and Sale in Africa

Extract from: John Barbot, "A Description of the Coasts of North and South Guinea," in Thomas Astley and John Churchill, ed., *Collection of Voyages and Travels* (1732).

*John Barbot, who was an agent for the French Royal African Trading Company, made two voyages to west Africa in the late seventeenth century. In this extract he describes how Africans were obtained for the slave trade and what happened to them before they were loaded on to the slave ships.*

Those sold by the Blacks are for the most part prisoners of war . . . others stolen away by their own countrymen; and some there are, who will sell their own children, kindred, or neighbours. . . . The kings are so absolute, that upon any slight pretense of offences committed by their subjects, they order them to be sold for slaves, without regard to rank, or possession. . . . The trade of slaves is in a more peculiar manner the business of kings, rich men, and prime merchants, exclusive of the inferior sort of Blacks.

As the slaves come down . . . from the inland country, they are put into a booth, or prison, built for that purpose, near the beach, all of them together; and when the Europeans are to receive them, every part of every one of them, to the smallest member, men and women being all stark naked. Such as are allowed good and sound, are set on one side, and the others by themselves; which slaves so rejected are . . . being above thirty five years of age, or defective in their limbs, eyes or teeth; or grown grey, or that have the venereal disease, or any other imperfection. These being set aside, each of the others, which have passed as good, is marked on the breast, with a red-hot iron, imprinting the mark of the French, English, or Dutch companies, that so each nation may distinguish their own, and to prevent their being chang'd by the natives for worse, as they are apt enough to do. In this particular, care is taken that the women, as tenderest, be not burnt too hard.

The branded slaves, after this, are returned to their former booth. . . . There they continue sometimes ten or fifteen days, till the sea is still enough to send them aboard; for very often it continues too boisterous for so long a time, unless in January, February and March, which is commonly the calmest season: and when it is so, the slaves are carried off by parcels . . . and put aboard the ships in the road. Before they enter the canoes, or come out of the booth, their former Black masters strip them of every rag they have, without distinction of men or women; to supply which, in orderly ships, each of them as they come aboard is allowed a piece of canvas, to wrap around their waist, which is very acceptable to those poor wretches.

### b. The Middle Passage

Extract from: Olaudah Equiano, *The Interesting Narrative of the Life of Olaudah Equiano or Gustavus Vassa the African* (1789).

*Olaudah Equiano was only eleven years old when he was kidnapped from his African village. In this extract from his autobiography he recalls his fright when he believed that the Europeans he was encountering for the first time intended to eat him. He goes on to record the appalling conditions on the slave ships.*

The first object which saluted my eyes when I arrived on the coast was the sea, and a slave-ship, which was then riding at anchor, and waiting for its cargo. These filled me with astonishment, which was soon converted into terror, which I am yet at a loss to describe, nor the then feelings of my mind. When I was carried on board I was immediately handled, and tossed up, to see if I were sound, by some of the crew; and I was now persuaded that I was got into a world of bad spirits, and that they were going to kill me. Their complexions too differing so much from ours, their long hair, and the language they spoke, which was very different from any I had ever heard, united to confirm me in this belief. Indeed, such were the horrors of my views and fears at the moment, that, if ten thousand worlds had been my own, I would have freely parted with them all to have exchanged my condition with that of the meanest slave in my own country.

When I looked round the ship too, and saw a large furnace of copper boiling, and a multitude of black people of every description chained together, every one of their countenances expressing dejection and sorrow, I no longer doubted of my fate, and, quite overpowered with horror and anguish, I fell motionless on the deck and fainted. When I recovered a little, I found some black people about me, who I believed were some of those who brought me on board, and had been receiving their pay; they talked to me in order to cheer me, but all in vain. I asked them if we were not to be eaten by those white men with horrible looks, red faces, and long hair? They told me I was not. . . .

Soon after this, the blacks who brought me on board went off, and left me abandoned to despair. I now saw myself deprived of all chance of returning to my native country, or even the least glimpse of hope of gaining the shore, which I now considered as friendly: and I even wished for my former slavery in preference to my present situation, which was filled with horrors of every kind, still heightened by my ignorance of what I was to undergo.

I was not long suffered to indulge my grief; I was soon put down under the decks, and there I received such a salutation in my nostrils as I had never experienced in my life; so that with the loathsomeness of the stench, and crying together, I became so sick and low that I was not able to eat, nor had I the least desire to taste any thing. I now wished for the last friend, Death, to relieve me; but soon, to my grief, two of the white men offered me eatables; and, on refusing to eat, one of them held me fast by the hands, and laid me across, I think, the windlass, and tied my feet, while the other flogged me severely. I had never experienced any thing of this kind before; and although, not being used to the water, I naturally feared that element the first time I saw it; yet, nevertheless, could I have got over the nettings, I would have jumped over the side, but I could not; and, besides, the crew used to watch us very closely who were not chained down to the decks, lest we should leap into the water; and I have seen some of these poor African prisoners most severely cut for attempting to do so, and hourly whipped for not eating. This indeed was often the case with myself.

At last, when the ship we were in had got in all her cargo, they made ready with many fearful noises, and we were all put under deck, so that we could not see how they managed the vessel. But this disappointment was the least of my sorrow. The stench of the hold while we were on the coast was so intolerably loathsome, that it was dangerous to remain there for any time, and some of us had been permitted to stay on the deck for the fresh air; but now that the whole ship's cargo were confined together, it became absolutely pestilential. The closeness of the place, and the heat of the climate, added to the number in the ship, which was so crowded that each had scarcely room to turn himself, almost suffocated us. This produced copious perspirations, so that the air soon became unfit for respiration, from a variety of loathsome smells, and brought on a sickness among the slaves, of which many died, thus falling victims to the improvident avarice, as I may call it, of their purchasers. This wretched situation was again aggravated by the galling of the chains, now become insupportable; and the filth of the necessary tubs, into which the children often fell, and were almost suffocated. The shrieks of the women, and the groans of the dying, rendered the whole a scene of horror almost inconceivable. Happily perhaps for myself I was soon reduced so low here that it was thought necessary to keep me almost always on deck; and from my extreme youth I was not put in fetters. In this situation I expected every hour to share the fate of my companions, some of whom were almost daily brought upon deck at the point of death, which I began to hope would soon put an end to my miseries. Often did I think many of the inhabitants of the deep much more happy than myself; I envied them the freedom they enjoyed, and as often wished I could change my condition for theirs . . . [.] One day, when we had a smooth sea, and a moderate wind, two of my wearied countrymen, who were chained together (I was near them at the time), preferring death to such a life of misery, somehow made through the nettings, and jumped into the sea: immediately another quite dejected fellow, who, on account of his illness, was suffered to be out of irons, also followed their example; and I believe many more would soon have done the same, if they had not been prevented by the ship's crew, who were instantly alarmed. Those of us that were the most active were, in a moment, put down under the deck; and there was such a noise and confusion amongst the people of the ship as I never heard before, to stop her, and get the boat to go out after the slaves. However, two of the wretches were drowned, but they got the other, and afterwards flogged him unmercifully, for thus attempting to prefer death to slavery. In this manner we continued to undergo more hardships than I can now relate; hardships which are inseparable from this accursed trade.

## c. Rebellion

Extract from: John Barbot, "A Supplement to the Description of the Coasts of North and South Guinea," in Thomas Astley and John Churchill, ed., *Collection of Voyages and Travels* (1732).

*Here John Barbot describes an unsuccessful uprising that took place on board a slave ship during the Middle Passage.*

About one in the afternoon, after dinner, we, according to custom caused them, one by one, to go down between decks, to have each his pint of water; most of them were yet above deck, many of them provided with knives, which we had indiscreetly given them two or three days before, as not suspecting the least attempt of this nature from them; others had pieces of iron they had torn off our forecastle door, as having premeditated a revolt, and seeing all the ship's company, at best but weak and many quite sick, they had also broken off the shackles from several of their companions feet, which served them, as well as billets they had provided themselves with, and all other things they could lay hands on, which they imagin'd might be of use for this enterprize. Thus arm'd, they fell in crouds and parcels on our men, upon the deck unawares, and stabb'd one of the stoutest of us all, who receiv'd fourteen or fifteen wounds of their knives, and so expir'd. Next they assaulted our boatswain, and cut one of his legs so round the bone, that he could not move, the nerves being cut through; others cut our cook's throat to the pipe, and others wounded three of the sailors, and threw one of them over-board in that condition, from the fore-castle into the sea; who, however, by good providence, got hold of the bowline of the fore-sail, and sav'd himself . . . we stood in arms, firing on the revolted slaves, of whom we kill'd some, and wounded many: which so terrif'd the rest, that they gave way, dispersing themselves some one way and some another between decks, and under the fore-castle; and many of the most mutinous, leapt over board, and drown'd themselves in the ocean with much resolution, shewing no manner of concern for life. Thus we lost twenty seven or twenty eight slaves, either kill'd by us, or drown'd; and having master'd them, caused all to go betwixt decks, giving them good words. The next day we had them all again upon deck, where they unanimously declar'd, the Menbombe slaves had been the contrivers of the mutiny, and for an example we caused about thirty of the ringleaders to be very severely whipt by all our men that were capable of doing that office.

## d. Arrival

Extract from: Olaudah Equiano, *The Interesting Narrative of the Life of Olaudah Equiano or Gustavus Vassa the African* (1789).

*In this passage, Olaudah Equiano describes the way in which many newly arrived slaves were sold once they reached British America. He notes that it was at this point that family and friends could be permanently separated.*

As the vessel drew nearer, we plainly saw the harbor and other ships of different kinds and sizes and we soon anchored amongst them off Bridgetown. Many merchants and planters came on board. . . . They put us in separate parcels and examined us attentively. They also made us jump, and pointed to the land, signifying we were to go there. We thought by this we should be eaten by these ugly men, as they appeared to us. When soon after we were all put down under the deck again, there was much dread and trembling among us and nothing but bitter cries to be heard all the night from the apprehensions. At last the white people got some old slaves from the land to pacify us. They told us we were not to be eaten, but to work, and were soon to go on land, where we should see many of our country people. This report eased us much, and sure enough, soon after we landed, there came to us Africans of all languages.

We were conducted immediately to the merchant's yard, where we were all pent up together, like so many sheep in a fold, without regard to sex or age. . . . We were not many days in the merchant's custody, before we were sold after their usual manner. . . . On a signal given, (as the beat of a drum), buyers rush at once into the yard where the slaves are confined, and make a choice of that parcel they like best. The noise and clamor with which this is attended, and the eagerness visible in the countenances of the buyers, serve not a little to increase the apprehension of terrified Africans. . . . In this manner, without scruple, are relations and friends separated, most of them never to see each other again. I remember in the vessel in which I was brought over . . . there were several brothers who, in the sale, were sold in different lots; and it was very moving on this occasion, to see and hear their cries in parting.

## 3. Working Lives

### a. Plantation Work in Early-Eighteenth-Century Virginia

Extract from: Hugh Jones, *The Present State of Virginia* (1724).

*Reverend Hugh Jones, an Anglican minister who was based in Williamsburg, describes the work of enslaved people in early-eighteenth-century Virginia.*

Their work is to take care of the stock, and plant corn, tobacco, fruits, etc. which is not harder than thrashing, hedging, or ditching; besides, though they are out in the violent heat, wherein they delight, yet in wet or cold weather there is little occasion for their working in the fields, in which few will let them be abroad, lest by this means they might get sick or die, which would prove a great loss to their owners, a good Negroe being sometimes worth three (nay four) score pounds sterling, if he be a tradesman; so that upon this (if upon no other account) they are obliged not to overwork them, but to cloath and feed them sufficiently, and take care of their health.

Several of them are taught to be sawyers, carpenters, smiths, coopers, etc. and though for the most part they be none of the aptest or nicest; yet they are by nature cut out for hard labour and fatigue, and will perform tolerably well; though they fall much short of an Indian, that has learned and seen the same things; and those Negroes make the best servants, that have been slaves in their own country; for they that have been kings and great men there are generally lazy, haughty, and obstinate; whereas the others are sharper, better humoured, and more laborious.

### b. An Owner and His House Slaves in Early-Eighteenth-Century Virginia

Extract from: Louis B. Wright and Marion Tinling, ed., *The Secret Diary of William Byrd of Westover, 1709–1712* (1941).

*William Byrd (1674–1744), who traveled extensively in England and Europe, was one of early-eighteenth-century Virginia's most prominent planters and merchants. These entries from his diary show that the lives of house slaves could be far from easy.*

February 8, 1709 I rose at 5 o'clock this morning and read a chapter in Hebrew and 200 verses in Homer's Odyssey. I ate milk for breakfast. I said my prayers. Jenny and Eugene were whipped. . . .

February 22, 1709 I rose at 7 o'clock and read a chapter in Hebrew and 200 verses in Homer's Odyssey. I said my prayers and ate milk for breakfast. I threatened Anaka with a whipping if she did not confess the intrigues between Daniel and Nurse, but she prevented by a confession. I chided Nurse severely about it, but she denied, with an impudent face, protesting that Daniel only lay on the bed for the sake of the child.

June 10, 1709 George B-th brought home my boy Eugene . . . Eugene was whipped for running away and had the [bit] put on him. . . .

September 3, 1709 In the afternoon I beat Jenny for throwing water on the couch. . . .

December 1, 1709 Eugene was whipped again for pissing in bed and Jenny for concealing it. . . .

December 3, 1709 Eugene pissed abed again for which I made him drink a pint of piss.

June 17, 1710 In the afternoon I caused L-s-n to be whipped for beating his wife and Jenny was whipped for being his whore.

February 27, 1711 In the evening my wife and little Jenny had a great quarrel in which my wife got the worst but at last by the help of the family Jenny was overcome and soundly whipped.

### c. The Task System of the South Carolina and Georgia Lowcountry

Extract from: Johann Martin Bolzius, "Reliable Answer to Some Submitted Questions Concerning the Land Carolina," *The William and Mary Quarterly*, 14 (April 1957).

*Pastor Bolzius was the spiritual leader of a group of Lutheran migrants who settled in Georgia during the 1730s. In this letter to his superiors in Europe, he provides a detailed description of the task system that had developed in the rice-growing region of South Carolina.*

The order of planting is the following, 1) The Negroes plant potatoes at the end of March unless the weather is too cold. This keeps all Negroes busy, and they have to loosen the earth as much as they can. The potatoes are cut into several pieces and put into long dug furrows, or mounds, which are better than the former. When the leaves have grown 2 or 3 feet long (which is usually the case at the end of May or early June), one piles these leaves on long hills so that both ends project and are not covered. 2) As soon as one is through with the potatoes, one plants Indian corn. A good Negro man or woman must plant half an acre a day. Holes are merely made in the earth 6 feet from one another, and 5 or 6 kernels put into each hole. 3) After the corn the Negroes make furrows for rice planting. A Negro man or woman must account for a quarter acre daily. On the following day the Negroes sow and cover the rice in the furrows, and half an acre is the daily task of a Negro. 4) Now the Negroes start to clean the corn of the grass, and a day's work is half an acre, be he man or woman, unless the ground is too full of roots. 5) When they are through with that, they plant beans together among the corn. At this time the children must weed out the grass in the potato patches. 6) Thereupon they start for the first time to cultivate the rice and to clean it of grass. A Negro must complete 1/4 acre daily. 7) Now the corn must be cleaned of the grass for the second time, and a little earth put around the stalks like little hills. Some young corn is pulled out, and only 3 or 4 stalks remain. A little earth is also laid on the roots of the beans, all of which the Negroes do at the same time. Their day's task in this work is half an acre for each. 8) As soon as they are through with the corn, they cultivate the rice a second time. The quality of the land determines their day's work in this. 9) Corn and rice are cultivated for the third and last time. A Negro can take care of an acre and more in this work, and 1/4 an acre of rice. Now the work on rice, corn, and beans is done. As soon as the corn is ripe it is bent down so that the ears hang down towards the earth, so that no water collects in them or the birds damage them.

Afterwards the Negroes are used for all kinds of house work, until the rice is white and ripe for cutting, and the beans are gathered, which grow much more strongly when the corn has been bent down. The rice is cut at the end of August or in September, some of it also early in October. The pumpkins, which are also planted among the corn, are now ripening too. White beets are sown in good fertilized soil in July and August, and during the full moon. Towards the middle of August all Negro men of 16 to 60 years must work on the public roads, to start new ones or to improve them, namely for 4 or 5 days, or according to what the government requires, and one has to send along a white man with a rifle or go oneself. At the time when the rice is cut and harvested, the beans are collected too, which task is divided among the Negroes. They gather the rice, thresh it, grind it in wooden mills, and stamp it mornings and evenings. The corn is harvested last. During the 12 days after Christmas they plant peas, garden beans, transplant or prune trees, and plant cabbage. Afterwards the fences are repaired, and new land is prepared for cultivating.

# 4. Family Lives

## a. Marriage

Extract from: John Brickell, *The Natural History of North Carolina. With an Account of the Trade, Manners, and Customs of the Christian and Indian Inhabitants* (1737).

*This extract from Brickell's description of the environment and peoples of North Carolina provides a rare account of a slave marriage ceremony.*

Their Marriages are generally performed amongst themselves, there being very little ceremony based upon that Head; for the Man makes the Woman a Present, such as a Brass Ring or some other Toy, which if she accepts of becomes his Wife; but if ever they part from each other, which frequently happens, upon any little Disgust, she returns his Present: These kinds of Contracts no longer binding them, than the woman keeps the pledge give her.

## b. Separation

*The most common ways in which slaves were separated from their immediate family members and friends was by being given away in their owners' last wills and testimonies or by being sold. In the first extract John Woolman notes the willingness of southern slave owners to break up slave families; in the second, John Sandefor bequeaths slaves to his sons. The final source shows the way in which owners often advertised slaves they wished to sell.*

Extract from: John Woolman, *Journal* (1774).

Many of the white people in those provinces take little or no care of Negro marriages; and when Negroes marry after their own way, some make so little account of those marriages that with views of outward interest they often part men from their wives by selling them far asunder, which is common when estates are sold.

Extract from: *Last Will and Testament of John Sandefur of Elizabeth City County, Virginia, 1742, Elizabeth County Deed & Will Book, 1737–1749.*

Know all men by these present that John Sandefur of Elizabeth City County, Virginia have for divers good causes and considerations me there unto especially moving I do by these present give unto my sons Robert and William and Peter one negro boy and three negro girls, that is to say my negro girl Sarah now give unto my son Robert Sandefur and all my goods that my son Robert has in his possession, I also give unto my son William, one negro girl named Judy. I also give unto my son Peter one negroe girl named Lucy and one negroe boy named Ned. Now the above mentioned negroes given to my said three sons Robert, William and Peter unto each and ever of them their heirs and assigns forever. Signed 16 Feb. 1742. His **X** mark John Sandefur In the presence of Wm. Davis; William Williams; Samuel Markoom

Extract from: *The South-Carolina and America Gazette,* 11–18 November 1771.

A Healthy, young NEGRO WENCH, is to be sold reasonable, and Rice taken in Payment, any Time within two Months. She may be deemed little more than a new Negro, as she was imported this Summer, talks rather plain, is very handy in the House, and at her Needle, without Fault or Blemish, and promises to be an able, stout Wench. The Owner, who is the only one she ever had, has too many, and which is really the only Reason of her being sold. Enquire Robert Wells [Printer]

**c. Domestic Economies**

Extract from: Johann Martin Bolzius, "Reliable Answer to Some Submitted Questions Concerning the Land Carolina," *The William and Mary Quarterly,* 14 (April 1957).

*Pastor Bolzius describes the housing, food, and gardens of enslaved people on a typical lowcountry rice plantation.*

*Housing:* They live in huts, each family, or 2 persons in one hut. The barn is built about 600 feet away from the house of the master and the huts of the

Negroes are arrayed around the barn, at a little distance from one another so that if fire breaks out in one hut the others are more easily saved. The costs of such a Negro hut are very minor. One buys only a few nails for them.

*Food:* From September to March their food is commonly potatoes and small unsalable rice, also at times Indian corn; but in summer corn and beans which grow in the plantation. Men, women, and children have the same food.

*Gardens:* They are given as much land as they can handle. On it they plant for themselves corn, potatoes, tobacco, peanuts, water and sugar melons, pumpkins, bottle pumpkins (sweet ones and stinking ones which are used as milk and drink vessels and for other things). They plant for themselves also on Sundays. . . . They sell their own crops and buy some necessary things.

Extract from: Philip Hamer, George C. Rogers, David R. Chesnutt et al., ed., *The Papers of Henry Laurens* (1968–).

*Henry Laurens was a prominent South Carolinian merchant and planter. In this letter he offers to provide his slaves with the goods they want in exchange for the rice they grew in their own time. His intention is to control the trading activities of his slaves.*

Henry Laurens to Abraham Schad (Overseer) April 30, 1765

With this I inclose you an account of sundry articles sent to be disposed among the Negroes for their Rice at the prices mark'd to each article which I hope they will take without too much fuss & trouble that I may not be discouraged from being their Factor another year. Their several names are set down & your quantity of each one's Rice on the credit side at 7/6 per Bushel, which is its full value & opposite to that you must make them Debtor for such goods as they take.

# 5. Religious Lives

## a. Anglican Missionary Activity in Early Eighteenth- Century South Carolina

Extract from: Frank J. Klingberg, ed., *The Carolina Chronicle of Dr. Francis Le Jau, 1706–1717* (1956).

*Reverend Francis Le Jau was an Anglican missionary employed by the Society for the Propagation of the Gospel in early-eighteenth-century South Carolina. In this letter he describes the difficulties he was encountering in his attempt to convert enslaved Africans to Christianity.*

Goose Creek, South Carolina, December 11, 1712. I thought to have baptized some more Negro Slaves this Advent they are well Instructed and I hear no complaint concerning them. Their Masters Seem very much Averse to my Design, Some of them will not give them Leave to come to Church to learn how to Pray to God & to Serve him, I cannot find any reason for this New Opposition but the Old pretext that Baptism makes the Slaves proud and Undutifull. I endeavour to convince them of the Contrary From the Example of those I have baptized, and Chiefly those who are Admitted to our holy Communion who behave themselves very well.

**b. Religious Transformation**

Extract from: Samuel Davies, *LETTERS From The Reverend Samuel Davies. Shewing The State of Religion in Virginia, particularly among the Negroes* (1757).

*In this extract, Reverend Samuel Davies, a Presbyterian minister who was based in Hanover County, Virginia, reports his success in converting enslaved people to Christianity.*

The number that attend upon my ministry at particular times is uncertain; but, I think, there are about three hundred that give a stated attendance. And never have I been so struck with the appearance of an assembly, as when I have glanced my eyes to one part of the meeting-house adorned (so it has appeared to me) with so many black Countenances, especially attentive to every word they heard, and some of them washed with tears. A considerable number of them (about an hundred) have been baptized . . . and given credible evidence, not only of their acquaintance with the important doctrines of the Christian Religion, but also a deep sense of these things upon their spirits, and a life of the strictest Morality and Piety. As they are not sufficiently polished to dissemble with a good grace, they express the sensations of their minds so much in the language of simple nature, and with such genuine indications of Sincerity, that it is impossible to suspect the profession of some of them, especially when attended by a regular behaviour in common life.

My worthy friend Mr. Todd, a Minister of the next congregation, has near the same number of Negroes under his pastoral charge; and some of them, he tells me, discover the same serious turn of mind. In short, there are multitudes of them in various parts, who are willing, and even eagerly desired to be instructed, and to embrace every opportunity for that end.

### c. Ancestral Retentions

Extract from: William D. Piersen, *Black Yankees: The Development of an Afro-American Subculture in Eighteenth-Century New England* (1988).

*This is an anonymous account from mid-eighteenth-century New England of the persistence of the African belief that after death the soul returned to Africa. Because of this, death was an occasion for joy rather than sorrow.*

She fully expected at death, or before, to be transported back to Guinea, and all her long life she was gathering, as treasures to take back to her motherland, all kinds of odds and ends, colored rags, bits of finery, peculiar shaped stones, shells, buttons, beads, anything she could string. Nothing came amiss to her store.

The funeral rites of a slave are performed by his brethren with every mark of joy and gladness—They accompany the corpse with every mark of joy and gladness—They accompany the corpse with the sound of musical instruments—They sing their songs and perform their dances around the grave and indulge themselves in mirth and pleasantry.

# 6. Resistance and Rebellion

### a. Punishment and Deterrence

Extract from: John Brickell, *The Natural History of North Carolina. With an Account of the Trade, Manners, and Customs of the Christian and Indian Inhabitants* (1737).

*John Brickell (1710–1745) was an Irishman who went to North Carolina in 1724. In this extract from his travel account, he describes the punishment of slaves who physically assaulted their owners or other whites.*

There are several laws made against them in this province to keep them in subjection, and particularly one, *viz.*, that if a Negroe cut or wound his master or a Christian with any unlawful weapon . . . and there is blood-shed, if it is known amongst the planters, they immediately meet and order him to be hanged, which is always performed by another Negroe, and generally the planters bring most of their Negroes with them to behold their fellow Negro suffer, to deter them from the vile practice.

## b. Rebellion

*The first extract is an eyewitness account of the Stono rebels provided by Lieutenant Governor Bull, who encountered them quite by chance. The second extract shows that not all slaves supported the rebels and provides details of the kinds of rewards that were offered to those who were prepared to betray them. The third source gives the most detailed account of the alleged slave conspiracy that shook New York City in 1741. It was written by Daniel Horsmanden, who was one of the justices involved in the trial of the supposed conspirators.*

Extract from: *Lieutenant Governor William Bull's account of the Stono Rebellion, 1739.*

On the 9th of September last at Night a great Number of Negroes Arose in Rebellion, broke open a Store where they got arms, killed twenty one White Persons, and were marching the next morning in a Daring manner out of the Province, killing all they met and burning several Houses as they passed along the Road. I was returning from Granville County with four Gentlemen and met these Rebels at eleven o'clock in the forenoon and fortunately deserned the approaching danger time enough to avoid it, and to give notice to the Militia who on the Occasion behaved with so much expedition and bravery, as by four a'Clock the same day to come up with them and killed and took so many as put a stop to any further mischief at that time, forty four of them have been killed and Executed; some few yet remain concealed in the Woods expecting the same fate, seem desperate.

Extract from: *A South Carolina Commons House of Assembly Committee Report in a Message to the Governor's Council, November 29, 1739.*

That upon Inquiry your Committee find that a negro man named July belonging to Mr. Thomas Elliott was very early and chiefly instrumental in saving his Master and his Family from being destroyed by the Rebellious Negroes and that the Negro man July had at several times bravely fought against the Rebels and killed one of them. Your Committee therefore recommends that the [said] Negro July (as a reward for his faithful Services and for an Encouragement to other Slaves to follow his Example in case of the like

Nature) shall have his Freedom and a Present of a Suit of Cloaths, Shirt, Hat, a pair of stockings and a pair of Shoes.

That the several Slaves hereafter named Ralph, Prince, Joe, Larush and Pompey belonging to the [said] Mr. Thos Elliott, Sampon belonging to Mr. Wilkinson, two Negro Men and a Negro Woman . . . belonging to Mr. Thomas Rose, Two Negro Men . . . who belong to the Estate of Mr. John Haynes decd. And one Negro Man . . . belonging to the Estate of Mr. Christopher Wilkinson decd a Negro man belonging to Mrs. Wilkson Widow named Mingo; a Mustee Man have behaved themselves very well and been a great source in opposing the Rebellions Negroes; For which your Committee recommend that they be rewarded as follows (that is to say) the Men to have each a Suit of Cloths, hat, shirt, a pair of Shoes, and a pair of Stockings, And the Women to have each a Jacket and Petticoat, a Shift, a pair of Stockings, and a pair of Shoes and also the sum of 20[lb] in Cash to each of the Slaves above named. . . .

That several of the Neighbouring Indians did assist in hunting for, taking and destroying the [said] Rebellious Negroes, For which your Committee propose that the [said] Indians be severally rewarded with a Coat, a Flap, a Hat, a pair of Indian Stockings, a Gun, 2 pounds of Powder and 8 Pounds of Bullets.

Extract from: Daniel Horsmanden, *Court Journal, New York, 1741.*

Wednesday, March 18 [1741] About one o'clock this day a fire broke out of the roof of his majesty's house at Fort George, within this city, near the chapel; when the alarm of fire was first given, it was observed from the town, that the middle of the roof was in a great smoke, but not a spark of fire appeared on the outside for a considerable time. . . . Upon the chapel bell's ringing, great numbers of people, gentlemen and others, came to the assistance of the lieutenant governor and his family; and . . . most of the household goods, etc. were removed and saved. . . . But the fire got hold of the roof . . . and an alarm being given that there was gun powder in the fort, whether through fear and an apprehension that there was, or whether the hint was given by some of the conspirators themselves, with artful design to intimidate the people, and frighten them from giving further assistance, we cannot say; though the lieutenant governor declared to every body that there was none there. . . .

Monday, April 6 [1741] About ten o'clock in the morning, there was an alarm of a fire at the house of serjeant Burns, opposite fort Garden. . . . Towards noon a fire broke out in the roof of Mrs. Hilton's house. . . . Upon view, it was plain that the fire must have been purposely laid. . . . There was a cry among the people, the Spanish Negroes; the Spanish Negroes; take up the Spanish Negroes. The occasion of this was the two fires . . . happening so closely together . . . and it being known that Sarly had purchased a Spanish Negro, some time before brought into his port, among several others . . . and that they afterwards pretending to have been free men in their country, began to grumble at their hard usage, of being sold as slaves. This probably gave rise to the suspicion, that this Negro, out of revenge, had been the instrument of these two fires; and he behaving insolently upon some people's asking him questions concerning them . . . it was told to a magistrate who was near, and he ordered him to jail, and also gave direction to constables to commit all the rest of that cargo [of Africans], in order for their safe custody and examination. . . . While the justices were proceeding to examination, about four o'clock there was another alarm of fire. . . . While the people were extinguishing the fire at this storehouse, and had almost mastered it, there was another cry of fire, which diverted the people attending the storehouse to the new alarm . . . but a man who had been on the top of the house assisting in extinguishing the fire, saw a Negro leap out at the end window of one of them . . . which occasioned him to cry out . . . that the Negroes were rising.

Supreme Court Wednesday, April 22 [1741] Deposition, No. 1—Mary Burton [a servant], being sworn, deposeth, 1. "That Prince [Mr. Auboyneau's slave] and Caesar [Mr. Varack's slave] brought the things which they had robbed . . . to her master, John Hughson's house . . . about two or three o'clock on a Sunday morning [March 1, 1740]. 2. That Caesar, Prince and Mr. Philipse's Negro man (Cuffee) used to meet frequently at her master's house, and that she had heard them (the Negroes) talk frequently of burning the fort; and that they would go down to the Fly [the city's east end] and burn the whole town; and that her master and mistress said, they would aid and assist them as much as they could. 3. "That in their common conversation they used to say, that when all this was done, Caesar should be governor, and Hughson, her master, should be king. 4. "That Cuffee used to say, that a great many people had too much, and others too little; that his old master had a great deal of money, but that, in a short time, he should have less, and that he (Cuffee) should have more. . . . 7. "That she had known at times, seven or eight guns in her master's house and some swords, and that she had seen twenty or thirty Negroes at one time in her master's house . . ." [.] This evidence of a conspiracy, not only to burn the city, but also destroy and murder the people, was most astonishing to the grand jury, and that any white people should become so abandoned as to confederate with slaves in such an execrable and detestable purpose, could not but be very amazing to every one that heard it. . . . [A Justice administers the sentence to Quack and Cuffee] You both now stand convicted of one of the most horrid and detestable pieces of villainy, that ever satan instilled into the heart of human creatures to put in practice; ye, and the rest of your colour, though you are called slaves in this country; yet are you all far from the condition of other slaves in other countries; nay, your lot is superior to that of thousands of white people. You are furnished with all the necessaries of life, meat, drink, and clothing, without care, in a much better manner than you could provide for yourselves, were you at liberty; as the miserable condition of many free people here of your complexion might abundantly convince you. What then could prompt you to undertake so vile, so wicked, so monstrous, so execrable and hellish a scheme, as to murder and destroy your own masters and benefactors? nay, to destroy root and branch, all the white people of this place, and to lay the whole town in ashes. I know not which is more astonishing, the extreme folly, or wickedness, of so base and shocking a conspiracy. . . . What could it be expected to end in, in the account of any rational and considerate person among you, but your own destruction?

### c. Individual Acts of Violence

Extract from: T. G. Tappert and J. W. Doberstein, ed. and trans., *The Journals of Henry Melchior Muhlenberg* (1942–1958).

*Henry Melchior Muhlenberg was a prominent German Lutheran who visited Georgia and South Carolina on the eve of the American Revolution. In this extract from his travel journal, he describes the attempted murder of Pastor Rabenhorst and his wife, who were also Lutherans, by one of their female house slaves.*

Savannah, Georgia, 1774

One evening an old sullen house Negress had taken some arsenic, which she had been using to kill rats, and put it into the coffee, seeking to kill her master and mistress. As soon as Mr. Rabenhorst drank the first cup of it he became dizzy and sick and had to vomit. Mrs. R, supposing it to be caused by something else, also drank a cup, whereupon she immediately suffered the same violent effects. When the contents of the coffee-pot were examined, the poison was discovered in the grounds. They were in extreme peril of death, but by God's grace were saved by the use of powerful medicines. The Negress is said to have betrayed herself by saying to the other Negress, I thought my master and mistress would get enough, but it was not sufficient. The Negress fell into the hands of the authorities, was condemned, and after several weeks burned alive.

#### d. Gendered Resistance in the Workplace

Extract from: Jack P. Greene, ed., *The Diary of Colonel Landon Carter of Sabine Hall, 1752–1778* (1965).

*Landon Carter was one of Virginia's wealthiest planters. In this extract from his diary, he shows some of the ways in which slave women used their bodies to gain some relief from the often backbreaking work involved in plantation agriculture. He also indicates the punishments they faced when their ruses were discovered.*

[1770]

The two Sarah's came up yesterday pretending to be violently ill with pains in their sides. They looked very well, had no fever, and I ordered them down to their work upon pain of a whipping. They went, worked very well with no grunting about pain but one of them, Manuel's Sarah, taking advantage of Lawson's ride to the Fork, swore she would not work any longer and ran away and is still out. There is a curiosity in this creature. She worked none last year pretending to be with child and this she was full 11 months before she was brought to bed. She has now the same pretense and thinks to pursue the same course but as I have full warning of her deceit, if I live, I will break her of that trick. I had two before of this turn. Wilmot of the Fork whenever she was with child always pretended to be too heavy to work and it cost me twelve months before I broke her. Criss of Mangorike fell into the same scheme and really carried it to a great length for at last she could not be dragged out. However by carrying a horse with traces the lady took to her feet ran away and when caught by a severe whipping has been a good slave ever since only a cursed thief in making her children milk my cows at night.

#### e. Runaways

Extracts from: *Colonial newspapers*.

*One of the main ways in which owners in both the northern and the southern colonies tried to reclaim enslaved runaways was by advertising for their capture and* return in colonial newspapers. These advertisements show the kind of information that owners supplied about their slaves, and also give some indication about the ways in which they treated them.

The South Carolina Gazette, August 13, 1737.

RUN AWAY from the Plantation of Isaac Porcher on Wassamsaw, a new Angola Negro Man, named Clawss, he is a small Fellow, and very black, he had on when he went away a Breeches, Jacket and Cap of white Plains, pretty much worn and dirty, any Person who shall apprehend the said Negro Man, and bring him to his Master, or to Goal in Charlestown, or give Information so as he may be had again, shall receive 2 [lb] reward and all Charges paid by Isaac Porcher. N.B. As there is abundance of Negroes in the Province of that Nation, he may chance to be harbour'd among some of them, therefore all Masters are desired to give notice of their Slaves who shall receive the same reward, if they take up the said Runaway.

The Pennsylvania Gazette, December 19, 1765.

Went away from Joseph Sharp, of Salem County, West Jersey, the 10th Day of November last, a Negroe Man, named Sambo, under Pretence to get a Master; he is a thick short Fellow, limps with his Right Knee, and one of his Buttocks, bigger than the other, about 40 Years of Age, talks much, and cannot count above 15, if you ask him how much 10 and 5 is he can't tell such Question; he has had many Masters, and lived at Mount Holly, when the Furnace went, with Mr. Baird; it is thought will endeavour to get to Philadelphia, or is gone to New York. Whoever takes up the said Negroe, and secures him in any Gaol, so that his Master may have him again, shall have Three Pounds Reward; if taken in the County of Cumberland, Forty Shillings, paid by JOSEPH SHARP.

The Georgia Gazette, July 13, 1774.

RUN AWAY from the subscriber, A NEGROE WENCH, named FLORA, very well known in Savannah, has a scar of an old burn on her left arm; and likewise one on her temple, and a scar of a whip on her right arm; she is supposed be harboured under the Bluff by sailors, as she has been frequently seen about the wharves and shipping: These are therefore to forewarn all Masters of vessels from harbouring or carrying off the said Negroe, as they may depend upon being prosecuted to the utmost rigour of the law. . . . ELIZABETH DEVEAUX.

# 7. Critiques and Defenses of
# Slavery and the Transatlantic
# Slave Trade

## a. Early Quaker Opposition to Slavery and the Transatlantic Slave Trade

Extract from: *The Germantown Petition, 1688.*

*This is the first recorded opposition to black slavery anywhere in British America. Note that these Quaker petitioners are comparing their own persecution in Europe with that of enslaved Africans.*

There is a saying, that we should do to all men like as we will be done ourselves; making no difference of what generation, descent, or colour they are. . . . To bring men hither, or rob and sell them against their will, we stand against. In Europe there are many oppressed for conscience-sake; and here there are those oppressed which are of a black colour. . . . Pray, what thing in the world can be done worse towards us, than if men should rob or steal us away, and sell us for slaves to strange countries; separating husbands from their wives and children.

## b. The Dispute between Samuel Sewall and John Saffin

Extracts from: Samuel Sewall, *The Selling of Joseph: A Memorial* (1700) and John Saffin, *A Brief and Candid Answer to the late Printed Sheet, Entituled, The Selling of Joseph* (1701).

*In 1700 two Massachusetts lawyers, Samuel Sewall and John Saffin, fell out over a case involving a black slave owned by Saffin. This prompted Sewall to write a pamphlet criticizing slavery and the slave trade. A year later Saffin challenged Sewall's antislavery arguments. These extracts show how both men used the Bible to justify their opposing positions.*

*Samuel Sewall*

Forasmuch as liberty is in real value next to life, none ought to part with it themselves, or deprivate others of it, but upon most mature consideration. The numerousness of slaves at this day in the province, and the uneasiness of them under their slavery, has put many upon thinking whether the foundation of it be firmly and well laid, so as to sustain the vast weight that is built upon it. It is most certain that all men, as they are the sons of Adam, are coheirs, and have equal right unto liberty, and all other outward comforts of life . . . all things considered, it would conduce more to the welfare of the province to have white servants for a term of years than to have slaves for life. Few can endure to hear of a Negro's being made free, and indeed they can seldom use their freedom well; yet their continual aspiring after their forbidden liberty renders them unwilling servants and there is such a disparity in their conditions, color, and hair that they can never embody with us and grow up into orderly families, to the peopling of land, but still remain in our body politic as a kind of extravasat[ed] blood. . . .

It is likewise most lamentable to think, how in taking Negroes out of Africa and selling of them here, that which God has joined together men do boldly rent asunder—men from their wives, parents from their children. How horrible is the uncleanness, mortality, if not murder, that the ships are guilty of that bring great crowds of these miserable men and women. Methinks, when we are bemoaning the barbarous usage of our friends and kinfolk in Africa, it might not be unseasonable to inquire whether we are not culpable in forcing the Africans to become slaves among ourselves.

*John Saffin*

The sum of [*Sewall's*] long Harangue, is no other, than to compare the Buying and Selling Of Negro's unto the Stealing of men, and the Selling of Joseph by his Brethren, which bears no proportion therewith, nor is there any congruity therein . . .

Our Author does further proceed to answer some Objections of his own framing, which he supposes some might raise.

Object. 1. That these Blackamores are of the Posterity of Cham, and therefore under the Curse of Slavery . . .

Ans. Whether they were or not, we shall not dispute: this may suffice, that not only the seed of Cham . . . but any lawful Captives of other Heathen Nations may be Bond men as hath been proved.

Object. 2. That the Negroes are brought out of Pagan Countreys into places where the Gospel is Preached. To which he Replies, that we must not doe Evil that Good may come of it.

Ans. To which we answer, That it is no Evil thing to bring them out of their own Heathenish Country, where they may have the Knowledge of the True God, be Converted and Eternally saved . . .

By all which it doth evidently appear both by Scripture and Reason, the practice of the People of God in all Ages, both before and after the giving of the Law, and in the times of the Gospel, that there were Bond men, Women and Children commonly kept by holy and good men, and improved in Service; and therefore by the Command of God, Lev. 24:44, and their venerable Example, we may keep Bond men, and use them in our Service still; yet with all candour, moderation and Christian prudence, according to their state and condition consonant to the Word of God.

### c. Opposition to the Introduction of Black Slavery to Georgia

A Petition to the Founders of Georgia, 1739

*In 1735 the British-based founders of Georgia persuaded the British Parliament to pass a law prohibiting black slavery in the colony. By 1739 this decision was provoking a storm of opposition in Georgia, with many settlers demanding permission to be able to use slaves. A few settlers, though, supported the decision to exclude slavery. Among them was a group of colonists who had emigrated to Georgia from the Highlands of Scotland. In 1739, eighteen of them petitioned Oglethorpe and the other Trustees urging that they maintain the ban on slavery.*

To his Excellency General Oglethorpe. The Petition of the Inhabitants of New Inverness

We are informed, that our Neighbors of Savannah, have petitioned your Excellency for the Liberty of having Slaves: We hope, and earnestly intreat, that before such Proposals are hearkened unto, your Excellency will consider our Situation, and of what dangerous and bad Consequence such Liberty would be of to us, for Many Reasons.

1. The Nearness of the Spaniards, who have proclaimed Freedom to all Slaves, who run away from their Masters, makes it impossible for us to keep them, without more Labour in guarding them, that what we would be at to do their Work.

2. We are laborious, and know a white Man may be, by the Year, more usefully employed than a Negroe.

3. We are not rich, and becoming Debtors for Slaves, in Case of their running away or dying, would inevitably ruin the poor Master, and he become a greater Slave to the Negroe-Merchant, than the Slave he bought could be to him.

4. It would oblige us to keep a Guard Duty at least as severe, as when we

expected a daily Invasion: And if that was the Case, how miserable would it be to us, and our Wives and Families, to have one enemy without, and a more dangerous one in our Bosom!

5. It is shocking to human Nature, that any Race of Mankind and their Posterity should be sentenc'd to perpetual Slavery; nor in Justice can we think otherwise of it, than that they are thrown amongst us to be our Scourge one Day or other for our Sins: And as Freedom must be as dear to them as to us, what a Scene of Horror must it bring about! And the longer it is unexecuted, the bloody Scene must be the greater. We therefore for our own Sakes, our Wives and Children, and our Posterity, beg your Consideration, and intreat, that instead of introducing Slaves, you'll put us in the Way to get some of our Countrymen, who, with their Labour in Time of Peace, and our Vigilance, if we are invaded, with the Help of those, will render it a difficult Thing to hurt us, or that part of the Province we possess. We will for ever pray for your Excellency, and are with all Submission, etc. Signed by eighteen Freeholders of New Inverness, in the District of Darien. January 1739.

### d. John Woolman

Extract from: John Woolman, *Journal* (1774).

*Beginning in the 1740s, John Woolman became a leading opponent of slavery and the slave trade. He used the Bible in support of his antislavery argument, but also emphasized the natural right to freedom of all humankind. Woolman was also one of the first writers to suggest that because slaves had no incentive to work in order to better themselves this meant that slavery was not as profitable as free labor.*

Soon after I entered this province [Maryland] a deep and painful exercise came upon me . . . as the people in this and the Southern Provinces live much on the labor of slaves, many of whom are used hardly. . . . We pursued our journey. . . . On the way we had the company of a colonel of the militia, who appeared to be a thoughtful man. I took occasion to remark on the difference in general betwixt a people used to labor moderately for their living, training up their children in frugality and business, and those who live on the labor of slaves; the former, in my view, being the most happy life. He concurred in the remark, and mentioned the trouble arising from the untoward, slothful disposition of the Negroes, adding that one of our laborers would do as much in a day as two of their slaves. I replied, that free men, whose minds were properly on their business, found a satisfaction in improving, cultivating, and providing for their families; but Negroes, laboring to support others who claim them as their property, and expecting nothing but slavery during life, had not the like inducement to be industrious. . . . I said . . . I believed that liberty was the natural right of all men equally. This he did not deny, but said the life of the Negroes were so wretched in their own country that many of them lived better here than there. . . . To which I replied, if compassion for the Africans, on account of their domestic troubles, was the real motive of our purchasing them, that spirit of tenderness being attended to, would incite us to use them kindly, that, as strangers brought out of affliction, their lives might be happy among us. And as they are human creatures, whose souls are as precious as ours . . . we could not omit suitable endeavors to instruct them therein; but that while we manifest by our conduct that our views in purchasing them are to advance ourselves, and while our buying captives taken in war animates those parties to push on the war, and increase desolation amongst them, to say they live unhappily in Africa is far from being an argument in our favor.

### e. Phillis Wheatley

Extract from: Phillis Wheatley, *Poems on Various Subjects, Religious and Moral* (1773).

*On the eve of the American Revolution, Phillis Wheatley was well known as a poet both in America and in England. Her poetry dealt with a wide range of religious, classical, and political subjects. In the first extract she deals with her capture and sale in Africa and removal to America. As the second extract shows, Phillis Wheatley believed that that there was a deep inconsistency between the colonists' demand for their own liberty and the continuation of black slavery.*

#### On being brought from A F R I C A to A M E R I CA.

'TWAS mercy brought me from my Pagan land,
Taught my benighted soul to understand
That there's a God, that there's a Saviour too:
Once I redemption neither sought nor knew,
Some view our sable race with scornful eye,
"Their colour is a diabolic die."
Remember, Christians, Negroes, black as Cain,
May be refin'd, and join th' angelic train.

*Phillis Wheatley to the Rev. Samson Occom, February 11, 1774, in The Connecticut Gazette, March 11, 1774.*

Reverend and honoured Sir,

I have this day received your obliging kind epistle, and am greatly satisfied with your reasons respecting the negroes, and think highly reasonable what you offer in vindication of their natural rights: Those that invade them cannot be insensible that the divine light is chasing away the thick darkness which broods over the land of Africa; and the chaos which has reigned so long, is converting into beautiful order, and reveals more and more clearly the glorious dispensation of civil and religious liberty, which are so inseparably united, that there is little or no enjoyment of one without the other: Otherwise, perhaps, the Israelites had been less solicitous for their freedom from Egyptian slavery; I do not say they would have been contented without it, by no means; for in every human breast God has implanted a principle, which we call love of freedom; it is impatient of oppression, and pants for deliverance; and by the leave of our modern Egyptians I will assert, that the same principle lives in us. God grant deliverance in his own way and time, and get him honour upon all those whose avarice impels them to countenance and help forward the calamities of their fellow creatures. This I desire not for their hurt, but to convince them of the strange absurdity of their conduct, whose words and actions are so diametrically opposite. How well the cry for liberty, and the reverse disposition for the exercise of oppressive power over others agree—I humbly think it does not require the penetration of a philosopher to determine.

By the law of nature, all persons are free. But absolute freedom is incompatible with civil establishments. Every man's liberty is restricted by national laws, and natural privilege does rightly yield to legal constitutions; which are designed and enacted for the public weal.

### f. Benjamin Rush and Bernard Romans: Anti- and Proslavery Arguments on the Eve of the American Revolution

Extracts from: Benjamin Rush, *An Address to the Inhabitants of the British Settlements in America, upon Slave-Keeping* (1773) and Bernard Romans, *A Concise History of East and West Florida* (1775).

*In 1773 Dr. Benjamin Rush of Philadelphia published an attack on slavery in which, among other things, he challenged the notion that Africans were naturally inferior to Europeans. Two years later Bernard Romans, who had been born in the Netherlands and went to America in 1755, where he worked as a civil engineer and botanist, replied to Rush's antislavery arguments. In the process he produced one of the most vigorous defenses of slavery, which tried to depict it as a "positive good" rather than a "necessary evil."*

*Benjamin Rush*

The design of the following address is to sum up the leading arguments against [slavery], several of which have not been urged by any of the authors who have written upon it. . . . I shall proceed immediately to combat the principal arguments which are used to support it.

And here I need hardly say any thing in favor of the Intellects of the Negroes, or of their capacities for virtue and happiness, although these have been supposed by some to be inferior to those of the inhabitants of Europe. The accounts which travelers give us of their ingenuity, humanity, and strong attachment to their parents, relations, friends and country, show us that they are equal to the Europeans. . . . But we are to distinguish between an African in his own country, and an African in a state of slavery in America. Slavery is so foreign to the human mind, that the moral faculties, as well as those of the understanding are debased, and rendered torpid by it. All the vices which are charged upon the Negroes in the southern colonies, and the West Indies, such as Idleness, Treachery, Theft, and the like, are the genuine offspring of slavery, and serve as an argument to prove, that they were not intended, by Providence, for it.

Nor let it be said, in the present Age, that their black color (as it is commonly called) either subjects them to, or qualifies them for slavery. The vulgar notion of their being descended from Cain, who was supposed to have been marked with this color, is too absurd to need a refutation. Without enquiring into the Cause of this blackness, I shall only add upon this subject, that so far from being a curse, it subjects the Negroes to no inconveniences, but on the contrary qualifies them for that part of the Globe in which providence has placed them. The ravages of heat, diseases and time, appear less in their faces than a white one; and when we exclude variety of color from our ideas of Beauty, they may be said to possess every thing necessary to constitute it common with the white people.

*Bernard Romans*

The very perverse nature of this black race seems to require the harsh treatment they generally receive, but like all other things, this is carried into the extreme; far be it from me to approve or recommend the vile usage to which this useful part of the creation is subjected by some of our western nabobs, but against the Phyllis [*Wheatley*] of Boston (who is the Phoenix of her race) I could bring at least twenty well known instances of the contrary effect of education on this sable generation.

Treachery, theft, stubbornness, and idleness . . . are such consequences of their manner of life at home as to put it out of all doubt that these qualities are natural to them, and not originated by their state of slavery. . . . I think no man ought to be allowed the manumission of his slave except he be bound for his good behaviour and industry, and idle free blacks ought to be sold for the good of the community . . .

Can any one say that the favourites of mankind (I mean liberty and property) are any where enjoyed in Africa? The rhapsodical opinion that the earth produced more when worked by free men than by slaves may do in theory but not in practice; the contrary is easily made to appear. . . .

It is pretended that our employing slaves is contrary to the precepts of the founder of our most holy religion, when he says: "*Thou shalt love thy neighbour as thyself*," I need not make use of the confined idea of the ancient Jews, who thought that the title of neighbour did not extend to any thing beyond their own nation.

I will then affirm, that there is a fivefold state of slavery, not only known or permitted; but commanded in God's holy word.

1st. Those who are condemned to slavery for their crimes, which we but too often experience to be the case with the slaves imported to us from Africa.

2ly. Those that are taken in war, which is the most general way among the Negroes to furnish us with slaves, and who would be murdered, did we not induce their conquerors by our manufactures and money to shew them mercy.

3ly. Those who are sold by their Parents, which custom obtains among many people even the refined and civilized Chinese, not to mention some christians, but most among the Negroes.

4ly. Those who sell themselves or are sold for debts, or other wants, which not only the Negroes, but our own laws justify.

5ly. Those who are born in slavery. . . .

It is not religion then nor christian charity that forbids us to have slaves, but it commands us the duties we are to fulfil towards them, instructing them to obey us, and us to use them as a part of the reasonable creation.

## g. Thomas Paine

Extract from: Thomas Paine, "African Slavery in America," *The Pennsylvania Journal and the Weekly Advertiser*, March 8, 1775.

*In this essay, published soon after he arrived in Pennsylvania from England, Thomas Paine challenged all the reasons used by the colonists to justify the enslavement of Africans.*

TO AMERICANS

That some desperate wretches should be willing to steal and enslave men by violence and murder for gain, is rather lamentable than strange. But that many civilized, nay, Christianized people should approve, and be concerned in the savage practice, is surprising; and still persist, though it has been so often proved contrary to the light of nature, to every principle of Justice and Humanity, and even good policy, by a succession of eminent men, and several late publications.

Our Traders in MEN (*an unnatural commodity!*) must know the wickedness of that SLAVE-TRADE, if they attend to reasoning, or the dictates of their own hearts; and such as shun and stifle all these, willfully sacrifice Conscience, and the character of integrity to that golden idol.

The Managers of that Trade themselves, and others, testify, that many of these African nations inhabit fertile countries, are industrious farmers, enjoy plenty, and lived quietly, adverse to war, before the Europeans debauched them with liquors, and bribing them against one another; and that these inoffensive people are brought into slavery, by stealing them, tempting Kings to sell subjects, which they have no right to do, and hiring one tribe to war against another. . . . By such wicked and inhuman ways the English are said to enslave towards one hundred thousand yearly . . .

Most shocking of all is alleging the Sacred Scriptures to favour this wicked practice. One would have thought none but infidel cavilers would endeavor to make them appear contrary to the plain dictates of natural light, and Conscience, in a matter of common Justice and Humanity, which they cannot be. . . . As much in vain, perhaps, will they search ancient history for examples of the modern Slave-Trade. Too many nations enslaved the prisoners they took in war. But to go to nations with whom there is no war . . . purely to catch inoffensive people, like wild beasts, for slaves, is an height of outrage against Humanity and Justice, that seems left by Heathen nations to be practiced by pretended Christians. How shameful are all attempts to colour and excuse it! As these people are not convicted of forfeiting freedom, they still have a natural, perfect right to it; and the Governments whenever they come should, in justice set them free, and punish those who hold them in slavery . . .

But the chief design of this paper is . . . to entreat Americans to consider. . . . With what consistency, or decency, they complain so loudly of attempts to enslave them, while they hold so many hundred thousands in slavery; and annually enslave many thousands more, without the pretence of authority, or claim upon them?

## 10.  An Offer of Freedom

Extract from: *Lord Dunmore's Proclamation, Virginia, 1775*

*In this extract, Lord Dunmore, the last Royal Governor of Virginia, offers enslaved men, but not enslaved women, belonging to Rebel planters their freedom in exchange for military service.*

As I have ever entertained Hopes that an Accommodation might have taken Place between GREAT-BRITAIN and this colony, without being compelled by my Duty to this most disagreeable but now absolutely necessary Step, rendered so by a Body of armed Men unlawfully assembled . . . and the formation of an Army, and that Army now on their March to attack His MAJESTY'S troops and destroy the well disposed Subjects of this Colony. To defeat such unreasonable Purposes, and that all such Traitors, and their Abetters, may be brought to Justice, and that the Peace, and good Order of this Colony may be again restored . . . I have thought fit to issue this my Proclamation, hereby declaring, that until the aforesaid good Purposes can be obtained, I do in Virtue of the Power and Authority to ME given, by His MAJESTY, determine to execute Martial Law, and cause the fame to be executed throughout this Colony: and to the end that Peace and good Order may the sooner be [effected], I do require every Person capable of bearing Arms, to [resort] to His MAJESTY'S STANDARD, or be looked upon as Traitors to His MAJESTY'S Crown and Government, and thereby become liable to the Penalty the Law inflicts upon such Offences; such as forfeiture of Life, confiscation of Lands, etc etc. And I do hereby further declare all indentured Servants, Negroes, or others, (appertaining to Rebels,) free that are able and willing to bear Arms, they joining His MAJESTY'S Troops as soon as may be, for the more speedily reducing this Colony to a proper Sense of their Duty.

# Bibliographic Essay

For many years the main focus of scholars who were interested in the history of slavery in early America was in the relative importance of race and economics in explaining the introduction of black slavery to the British American colonies. Two books were particularly significant in shaping this debate, Winthrop Jordan's *White over Black: American Attitudes toward the Negro, 1550–1812* (1968), and Edmund S. Morgan's *American Slavery, American Freedom: The Ordeal of Colonial Virginia* (1975). The ways in which race and economics interacted in the different seventeenth-century mainland colonies are also considered more briefly by Betty Wood in her *The Origins of American Slavery: Freedom and Bondage in the American Colonies* (1997).

Comparatively little has been written about slavery in the New England and Middle Atlantic colonies. The best studies of slavery in colonial New England are Lorenzo J. Greene, *The Negro in Colonial New England, 1620–1776* (1942); R. C. Twombly and R. H. Moore, "Black Puritan: The Negro in Seventeenth-Century New England," *William and Mary Quarterly* 3rd ser., 24 (1967): 224–42; and William D. Piersen, *Black Yankees: The Development of an Afro-American Subculture in Eighteenth-Century New England* (1988). For the Middle Atlantic colonies, see Charles L. Blockson, *Pennsylvania's Black History* (1975); Gary B. Nash, "Slaves and Slave Owners in Colonial Philadelphia," *William and Mary Quarterly* 3rd ser., 30 (1973): 223–56; Darold D. Wax, "The Demand for Slave Labor in Colonial Pennsylvania," *Pennsylvania Magazine of History and Biography* 34 (1967): 331–45; and Edgar McManus, *A History of Negro Slavery in New York* (1966 edition).

The more numerous studies of slavery in the colonial South are of two kinds: those that focus on a particular colony or colonies and those that favor a thematic approach. Virginia and South Carolina have attracted by far and away the most interest. The evolution of Virginia's slave society between the late seventeenth and the mid-eighteenth centuries is discussed by Allan Kulikoff in *Tobacco and Slaves: The Development of Southern Cultures in the Chesapeake, 1680–1800* (1986). Peter H. Wood's *Black Majority: Negroes in Colonial South Carolina from 1670 through the Stono Rebellion* (1974) remains a classic study of that colony. The slave societies of Virginia and South Carolina are compared in Philip D. Morgan's *Slave Counterpoint: Black Culture in the Eighteenth-Century Chesapeake and Lowcountry* (Chapel Hill, 1998). The best single work on slavery in colonial North Carolina is Marvin L. Michael Kay and Lorin Lee Cary's *Slavery in North Carolina, 1748–1775* (1995). Betty Wood examines the beginnings of slavery in Georgia in her *Slavery in Colonial Georgia, 1730–1775* (1984). For a rare attempt to provide an overview of slavery in early America, see Ira Berlin, *Many Thousands Gone: The First Two Centuries of Slavery in North America* (1998). Colonial laws relating to slavery are discussed in A. Leon Higginbotham Jr., *In The Matter Of Color: Race & The American Legal Process: The Colonial Period* (1978).

A great deal has been written about the transatlantic slave trade to the British American colonies. For the numbers of Africans shipped to America, and the mortality rates aboard the slave ships, see David Eltis and David Richardson, eds., *Routes to Slavery: Direction, Ethnicity and Mortality in the Atlantic Slave Trade* (1997). For studies that emphasize people rather than numbers, see Darold D. Wax, "Negro Resistance to the Early American Slave Trade," *Journal of Negro History* 15, I (1966): 1–15, and John K. Thornton, *Africa and Africans in the Making of the Atlantic World, 1400–1680* (1992). Planters' preferences for slaves from particular regions of Africa are discussed by Daniel C. Littlefield in *Rice and Slaves: Ethnicity and the Slave Trade in Colonial South Carolina* (1981).

The two main ways in which work was organized on large southern plantations, the gang system and the task system, are examined in Philip D. Morgan's "Task and Gang Systems: The Organization of Labor on New World Plantations," in Stephen Innes, ed., *Work and Labor in Early America* (1988). For the gendered distribution of tasks on plantations, see Carole Shammas, "Black Women's Work and the Evolution of Plantation Society in Virginia," *Labor History* 26 (1985): 5–28. Slaves' work in an urban setting is dealt with by Philip D. Morgan's "Black Life in Eighteenth-Century Charlestown," *Perspectives in American History* new series, 1 (1984): 187–232.

Important works that help us to better understand the formation of slave families and kinship networks include Russell R. Menard, "The Maryland Slave Population, 1685 to 1730: A Demographic Profile of Blacks in Four

Counties," *William and Mary Quarterly* 3d. ser., xxxii (January 1975); Allan Kulikoff, "The Beginnings of the Afro-American Family in Maryland," in Aubrey C. Land, Lois G. Carr, and Edward C. Papenfuse, eds., *Law, Society and Politics in Early Maryland* (1977); and Ira Berlin, "The Slave Trade and the Development of Afro-American Society in English Mainland America, 1619–1775," *Southern Studies* 20 (1981): 44–78. For the ways in which slave children were named in early America, see John C. Inscoe, "Carolina Slave Names: An Index to Acculturation," *Journal of Southern History* 49 (1983): 526–54, and Cheryl Ann Cody, "There was No 'Absalom' on the Ball Plantations: Slave-Naming Practices in the South Carolina Low Country, 1720–1865," *American Historical Review* 92 (1987): 563–96. For a recent study of the slaves' domestic economies, see Betty Wood, *Women's Work, Men's Work: The Informal Slave Economies of Lowcountry Georgia, 1750–1830* (1995).

Works on the religious lives of slaves in early America include Sylvia R. Frey and Betty Wood, *Come Shouting to Zion: African American Protestantism in the American South and British Caribbean to 1830* (1998). The persistence of African religious traditions is examined in Margaret Washington Creel's *"A Peculiar People": Slave Religion and Community Culture Among the Gullahs* (1988); Michael A. Gomez's "Muslims in Early America," *Journal of Southern History* 60 (1994): 671–700; and Richard Brent Turner's *Islam in the African-American Experience* (1994).

An influential early work on slave resistance was Gerald Mullins' *Flight and Rebellion: Slave Resistance in Eighteenth-Century Virginia* (1974). Most recent studies of slavery in individual colonies deal with different aspects of individual and group resistance. Peter Wood's *Black Majority* (1974) and John K. Thornton's "African Dimensions of the Stono Rebellion," *American Historical Review* 96 (1991): 1101–13, offer important insights into one of the most serious slave uprisings in Britain's mainland American colonies.

Critiques and defenses of slavery and the transatlantic slave trade in early America are examined in Lawrence W. Towner, "The Sewall-Saffin Dialogue on Slavery," *William and Mary Quarterly* 3d. ser., 21 (1964): 40–52; Jordan, *White over Black* (1968); and the opening chapters of Larry Tise, *Proslavery: A History of the Defense of Slavery in America, 1701–1840* (1987). For Phillis Wheatley, see David Grimsted, "Anglo-American Racism and Phillis Wheatley's 'Sable Veil,' 'Length'ned Chain,' and 'Knitted Heart,'" in Ronald Hoffman and Peter J. Albert, ed., *Woman in the Age of the American Revolution* (1989).

The beginning of the Revolutionary war in the southern mainland and its significance for slaves is dealt with in Sylvia R. Frey, *Water from the Rock:*

*Black Resistance in a Revolutionary Age* (1991). The ways in which the American Patriots tried to resolve the political and military problems posed by slavery are examined in David Brion Davis, *The Problem of Slavery in an Age of Revolution, 1770–1823* (1975) and Donald Robinson, *Slavery in the Structure of American Politics, 1765–1820* (1979).

# Index

Africans: equality of, 4–5; in Virginia, 8–9
agriculture, 7; labor in, 31–23
American Constitution, 59
American Revolution, 18, 51, 58, 59, 64
Anglicans: religious instruction of, 55–56;
  views on slavery of, 70–71. *See also* religion
apprenticeships, 38
arsenic, 64–65
arson, 65
Associates of the Late Reverend Dr.
  Thomas Bray, 56
Atlantic Ocean, Mariners' Chart of, *18*
Attucks, Crispus, 80
authority, 35–36
autobiographies, 49

Bacon, Nathaniel, 10
Bacon's Rebellion, 10, 62
Barbados, slave trade and, 5–6, 12
bartering, 47
Benezet, Anthony, 78; critiques of slavery
  of, 75, 76, 81
Berkeley, William, 10
Bible, 54; use of, to rationalize slavery,
  84–85
Bill of Rights, 84
Body of Liberties, 12–13

Boston Massacre, 80
branding, 20, 28; domination and, 29; initialed irons, *22*; methods of, 29
Bray, Thomas, 56
Brazil, 5
*A Brief and Candid Answer to a Late Printed
  Sheet, Entitled,* The Selling of Joseph
  (Saffin), 71
Britain: America and, 1–2; Holland and,
  17; Spain and, 16–17; territorial disputes of, 63; in transatlantic slave trade,
  20
Bull, William, 63
burials, African traditional, 50–51

Caribbean, 5
Carter, Robert, 82
Charleston, slave sale advertisements in,
  *28*
Chesapeake Bay, 1, 2, 32
childbearing, 44–45; naming traditions
  and, 45
Christianity, 6; bondage and, 70–71,
  72–73; conversion to, 53; imposition of,
  52; instruction in, 55; legal status and,
  10; spread of, 54–55. *See also* religion
class structure, 2
clothing, 66

127

~

# About the Author

**Betty Wood** is reader in American history at the University of Cambridge and a fellow at Girton College, Cambridge.